TIP
IT!

The World
According to Maggie

TIP IT!

MAGGIE GRIFFIN

HYPERION

NEW YORK

Library of Congress Cataloging-in-Publication Data has been applied for.

ISBN: 978-1-4013-2404-9

Hyperion books are available for special promotions and premiums. For details
contact the HarperCollins Special Markets Department in the New York office
at 212-207-7528, fax 212-207-7222, or email spsales@harpercollins.com.

Design by Sunil Manchikanti

FIRST EDITION

10 9 8 7 6 5 4 3 2 1

SUSTAINABLE FORESTRY INITIATIVE Certified Fiber Sourcing www.sfiprogram.org

THIS LABEL APPLIES TO TEXT STOCK

We try to produce the most beautiful books possible, and we are also extremely
concerned about the impact of our manufacturing process on the forests of the world
and the environment as a whole. Accordingly, we've made sure that all of the paper
we use has been certified as coming from forests that are managed, to ensure the
protection of the people and wildlife dependent upon them.

To my beloved husband, JOHN, and son KEN, who are no longer with me, and to JOYCE, GARY, JOHN M., and KATHY for your love and humor

Contents

TIP
IT!

OPENING

O h gosh, where do I begin?

The first thing you should know, readers, is that I don't really like to watch myself on my daughter Kathy's television show. I think I look different than I really look. My voice sounds different than I think it does. Seeing myself on television makes me hate the sound of my voice. I think I look and sound dumb.

Really, I think I look and sound crappy!

But then my friends or my kids tell me, "Well, that's you."

I know they don't mean the "crappy" part. I'm pretty sure what they mean is, I come off natural on television. Well, I've always had a good rapport with my youngest, my daughter Kathleen. I've certainly always felt natural with Kathy. At ease. But as you all may know, she loves saying things on television she knows I don't want to talk about. Certain things she does to provoke me, I could kill her for. And all that foul language! Christ. But I do the best I can. I go along with it. When you see me on *My Life on the D-List,* look at my body language, look how I sort of pull my arms and legs in close, getting ready for whatever she might say next; it must look like I'm warding off some impending storm when I'm on camera with her.

As long as I've watched her do stand-up, that moment has always come. She starts with, "Oh, I've got something to tell you about Maggie . . ." and it's all I can do not to try and figure out what it could possibly be she's going to tell about.

Usually all I can come up with is, "Oh my GOD, now what??"

I love Kathy, but I'm totally unlike her in many ways. First of all, I hate controversy. Hate it. I hate to hurt anyone's feelings. And I really like people. Mostly, I just like them to like me.

But when you watch Kathy imitate me in her act— all the swear words, the tough-sounding voice, and the complaining—even *I* get to thinking, "Gee, that Maggie really is a hard old dame!" Sometimes it's fun to play along. Some nice young kids recognized me recently, and they asked if they could take a picture of me. I said "Sure," and then they wanted to know if I'd flip them off for the camera. So I stuck my middle finger right out there and smiled. Well, why not? Maybe it's fun to have people think of ordinary wife and mom Maggie Griffin as being a little naughty once in a while!

People are generally really nice to me when they meet me out and about. They'll say, "I wish I had a mom like you!" Or "You're just like my mom!" And I think I know why. I'm a regular mom. I'm not a mother who pampers Kathy and caters to her. I love my daughter, and I'm immensely supportive of her, but hey, I tell her off. I know how to give her the business. I put her down. Not in a bad way, and I don't mean putting her down like a sick animal. That's a different kind of putting down. Again, I don't like to hurt people's feelings, but I'll say what needs to be said. "That was TERRIBLE, Kathy!" Or "I don't like that part!" Or "Enough already with the bad language."

Christ, that foul mouth gets old, Kathy.

Other times, when people on the street meet me, they refer to "your show." I may correct them—"Oh, it's not *my* show"—but I'll be a little devilish about it later and goad Kathy by telling her what they said. "Since when did it become 'My Life with Maggie Griffin'?" Kathy will say, and that makes me smile.

I get the whole thing about her giving me a hard time. Her goal is to provoke me, to confuse me, to rattle me, and let's face it, probably to make me look stupid. Then everybody laughs. It's very natural, what she and I do. Kathy doesn't make me mad, though, because I know why she's asking me those things. She's a comedian—a wonderful one, if I do say so myself—and if all I have to do is answer her the way I feel like answering her, and it's apparently funny, then fine.

My daughter Kathleen put out her memoir last year, *Official Book Club Selection*, which was real nice except for the controversial parts. But now I have a book. It's my turn, Kathy. I have some things to say, too, without having to be all controversial like you were. I have things to say about you. About me. About you *about* me. About where I came from. About the way the world has changed. About being a mom. About Hollywood. About wine. About *my* gays. About my dear departed husband, John Patrick Griffin. About how disgraceful children's clothes are these days. About how wonderful Bill O'Reilly is. That's right, Kathy. *Bill O'Reilly.* "My boyfriend," as you call him. He made you Pinhead of the Week once.

He got no argument from me.

In fact, he got a "Tip it!"

A NOTE SLIPPED IN BY KATHY

Hey everyone,

Maybe, like you, I picked up my mom's book hoping to find out how to be a tough, happy nonagenarian, for Chrissakes. Frankly, I also wanted to learn how she ended up getting a stronger gay fan base than I have.

But I've noticed that certain passages are—how shall I put this?—not entirely forthcoming about our relationship. Where I see my mother as a spotlight-hogging, wine-tipping muumuu wearer with a sailor's mouth, she sees herself as a good Catholic girl who through no fault of her own raised a potty-mouthed, trash-talking comedian who's shamed the family. This is the eternal struggle of our relationship, and—I'm guessing—isn't unlike a lot of mother-daughter relationships. And I guess when you get your own memoir, you're allowed to write what you want about yourself, and leave out the inconvenient parts, which I did not do in *Official Book Club Selection,* now available in paperback everywhere.

But since she's my mom—and since I know she's not going to reread her manuscript because she'd rather be watching *Judge Judy* or tippin' it—an opportunity arose for me to take a pen and add my two cents' worth without her ever noticing.

So I did.

Which means throughout this book, I've done only what I *had* to do as a concerned teller of dick jokes: crash the party, with my own "inconvenient" comments and observations. In some places I confront my mother outright. Think of *me* as Judge Judy when she has to get the truth out of a reluctant layabout. Or Nancy Grace when someone isn't paying enough attention to her twins.

There are plenty of sweet moments that need nothing from me, but other parts are just too crazy-sounding—I had to intervene.

So to use one of Maggie's favorite turns of phrase, I'll speak to you further!

XXOO
Kathy

YOU SAY MUUMUU,
I SAY DUSTER

*M*uumuu, duster, housedress, apron, caftan, smock, Mother Hubbard dress . . . Whatever you want to call it, I like to wear it. So sue me. [*Okay then, but the stretched-out Sears & Roebuck 1978 girdle underneath becomes Exhibit A.*] They're so darned comfortable and convenient [*so embarrassing when Mom swears like that*], no matter what Kathy says. Even back in my prime mothering days when women started to wear jeans and sweatshirts or T-shirts as their at-home clothing, I stuck with my dusters—which is what I always called them—because they were real handy. I'm not so modern, I guess, which is probably why my kids tease me about muumuus. [*So glad my mom wasn't one of those whore-moms who wore jeans.*]

When I was a kid, my mother wore a fresh pullover apron every day that was really like a dress. Sometimes she'd then put on another apron over that, the kind you tie in back. As I got older, though, you started to see aprons with snaps down the front, or zippers, that were easy to pull on, easy to pull off [*where is this going, Mom?*], and at the end of the day you could just throw it in the laundry. The name "duster," which is what I grew up with, says it all. You wore them while you did your dusting and other housework. [*Whew.*]

Let's face it, a woman needed something in between pajamas and dressy clothes if she was housebound but faced with the possibility of visitors at any moment. If a traveling salesman came to the door and you were wearing pajamas, that'd be far from nice. Not only would you be ill at ease, you might give a stranger unnecessary thoughts about you in the bedroom. [*Dear Penthouse Forum, I never thought this could happen to my mom . . .*] Well, there's nothing seductive about a duster. It's loose-fitting, presentable, and makes you look relaxed (even if you've just been on your hands and knees scrubbing away at a stain thanks to one of your damn kids).

Most of them had two big pockets, too! I could keep tissues, keys, whatever! Even a piece of banana bread if I were visiting a neighbor and she offered me one. [*In those days, "banana bread" was code for "wine."*]

Now, you always wore a bra and underpants underneath your duster. You may be indoors mostly, but there's no reason to be goofy. Also, hey, we lived in Chicago, where the winters got so bad, you sometimes had to wear pants under your duster to stay warm. That look wasn't so hot, I'll admit.

But who cares? You're not supposed to feel sexy. The idea was to be comfortable. Do you come home from work and throw on sweats and a T-shirt when you know you'll be in for the evening? Is that really any different? [*Whoa, take it down a notch, Miss Defensive.*]

Of course, Kathy would have you believe there was nothing else in my closet but muumuus. [*And one of my relatives in the clergy.*] But the most I've ever had was maybe five. That way I could wear one while another was in the wash. I tried real hard to find polyester or seersucker dusters, too, so I wouldn't even have to iron them! [*Sorry, Planet Earth!*]

As much as I love dusters, however, I was self-conscious about going to the store in one, even when the store was right up the street. I guess I thought it looked a little too domestic, like maybe I was there not just to shop, but to clean the shelves as well. Because remember, your duster wasn't always in great shape. Slipping out of one to put slacks and a jersey on was still pretty easy, though, so for an errand run I'd do that, and then as soon as the door to our house slammed shut behind me, it was back to the duster. But sometimes I'd be in the grocery aisle, and there'd be one of my neighbors, picking up a few items in her duster, and envy would set in.

"I wish I had those kind of guts," I'd think to myself.

In the end, whether they're around-the-house dusters or colorfully patterned muumuus like you see in Hawaii, they're addictive. [*Calling Dr. Drew.*] My best friends Irene and Rae and I often say that at our ages now, we'd love to be able to go out in our dusters instead of having to get dressed. Really, I could live in them, you know? [*Imagine a world . . .*]

Well, I've got a bombshell for you, readers. Kathy has not only worn one a few times—when she's been over and doesn't want to wrinkle her fancy clothes just sitting around, in which case I give her a duster to put on temporarily—but she also recently said something kinda shocking.

Referring to one of my simple, nice cotton dusters, she said to me, "Gee Ma, something like this would be kinda nice around the house." Excuse me, but isn't this the same woman who likes to portray my muumuus as some stamp of lazy, crotchety fashion sense? If I'd only had my darned camera those times she wore one! Somebody at *In Touch* would be getting a package in the mail. [*Why not Pony Express or mule train while you're at it?*]

See, I remember what it was like to go to the Groundlings and watch Kathy do a character based on me, wearing a muumuu and slippers and curlers. (And smoking, too. I never smoked! Where did that come from?) [*Breaking news: Every once in a while I exaggerate. Calling Nancy Grace.*] Of course, Kathy would never tell me when she'd taken a few from home for the act, and the first I'd know is sitting in the audience as she walked out onstage. If her uncle Maurice and aunt Mary knew how the nice muumuu they brought back from Hawaii was being portrayed, they'd have been furious!

And now we're at "Gee Ma, something like this would be kinda nice around the house." Has a nice ring, doesn't it? [*Snap! In my FACE!*]

Well, well, well. If being ninety has taught me anything, it's that the things you make fun of when you're younger, you find yourself embracing later on. We've all said it. "Oh God, I'm getting to be like my mother." Every girl's fear.

Anybody want to bet that my daughter changes her tune about muumuus *completely* and starts wearing them within ten years? [*I'm wearing one now, and going commando.*] Of course, the kind she gets won't be like mine. It'll be very, very expensive, probably, and handcrafted by some big shot designer so that you can't just throw it in the washer. Kathy will tell me how much she paid for it, and I'll shake my head and probably faint because I've never spent more than $12 on one. Then they'll become the rage, somebody will come up with a stupid name for them like mow-mows or moogly mooglies [*or an Hermès Birkin bag, but I digress*], and you'll have to spend a fortune for one that already looks faded and dirty and filled with holes, and then some poor cute starlet will be caught wearing one without anything on underneath and in some compromising position. [*For God's sake, Demi Lovato, zip up that muumuu!*]

Is nothing sacred? [*Nope.*]

One of my kids took this. Ha ha. But newspapers do keep you warm!

MAGGIE GRIFFIN

MUUMUU FUN FACTS

MUUMUU FUN FACT #1: Protestant missionaries first introduced the garment to Hawaiian women more than a century ago as a body-covering alternative to wearing grass skirts and showing their fofties everywhere!

MUUMUU FUN FACT #2: Drummer Jon Fishman of the scroungy rock band Phish has been known to wear one while performing, because it doesn't restrict his movement!

MUUMUU FUN FACT #3: The word "muumuu" stems from the Hawaiian word "mu'umu'u" which means "amputated"!

MUUMUU FUN FACT #4: "Muumuu" makes for a great word when you're stuck with all four "u" tiles in Scrabble! ("Tumultuous," too, but how likely is that?)

MY GAYS

When I say I get a lot of nice things said to me on the street, it's mostly from gay guys.

I still don't know a lot about homosexuals. And certain things about homosexuals I don't want to know. [*That's weird, because they're dying to hear about your sex life.*] But I've found they're such great people in a lot of ways. So many of them are delightful, they're very compassionate, and their sense of humor is fantastic. They're very creative, the gays. They're writers, artists, wonderful makeup artists, wonderful designers. [*I hear one time there was a gay attorney!*] Most of them make a damn good living and are really smart.

People are people, I say.

Now, at first, when we moved to Los Angeles, I have to admit I was surprised at how many were around. Kathy would have a party, say, and there'd be all these cute guys who were so adorable and funny, and I'd have such a good time talking to them about movies, show business, Judy Garland, whatever. [*Mostly Judy Garland.*]

I'd run over to my daughter and say, "Oh, Kathy, I just met this guy and he's so cute! Why don't you put the make on him?" [*Is that like taking a hit out on someone?*]

And she'd say, "Ma, he's gay."

"What?"

"He's gay."

Well, I just didn't know it! I couldn't tell, honest! I would just be laughing and talking with a guy and never catch on. [*Really, Mom? The quoting of lines from* The Wizard of Oz *didn't set off any bells?*] I don't know how many times I've had the "Ma, he's gay" conversation with Kathy. It seemed as if every cute guy at her parties was gay. Then again, the condo that my husband, Johnny, and I lived in in West Hollywood turned out to be half straight, half gay. We had these two fellas across the hall from us who were simply delightful, Randy and Steve. [*Can you still say "fellas," or is that considered un-PC?*] Very smart guys, one worked for the World Bank for years, and the other did something at UCLA. [*Hair?*] A teacher, I think he was. [*Oh.*] Anyway, one day I was talking to Randy, and I mentioned that I didn't think I'd ever known a gay guy until I'd moved out to California.

"Maggie," he said to me, "you knew them. You just didn't know they were gay."

And that was surely the truth! In our day it was this silent thing, and it had to have been awful for them. I always thought certain guys were just effeminate, or—God help me, this is the word we used then—sissies. [*Oh shit, here we go.*] And I just never got beyond that. I never knew what we're finding out now, that you're actually born gay. I thought you wanted to be gay. Really, that's what our generation thought. There was one kid I remember from high school—Jim [*I guarantee you, now it's James*] I'll call him since I don't really recall his name—who I'd pass by occasionally, and he'd have makeup on. [*Maggie's first drag queen!*]

I'd say, "Hi, Jim, how you doing?"

"Pretty good, Marge," he'd say.

Maybe I'd say, "Are you playing ball tonight?" [*Oh yeah, just not the kind you're thinking of, Marge.*] But that was really it. I'd wonder why he was wearing makeup, but I honestly didn't know then that gays sometimes wore it. Later, after I was married, there was a fella that Johnny worked with that people thought might have been gay. He was good-looking, a darling guy, and he came to all the parties. And I remember later, he would bring a guy to some of our parties, and this guy he brought was very, very out. He might have described him as a "buddy" or a "friend." But he was so cute, I'd always ask if he'd found a girlfriend. I'll be honest, I was very dumb about gays then.

Better-Looking Than All the Girls

KATHY: Mom, let me ask you something. When I was "dating" Tom Murphy in high school, who is now out and proud and has a nice boyfriend, did you ever think Tom was gay?

MAGGIE: Never. As God is my judge. All I knew was, I always thought he was so cute. Remember when you guys were in that *Babes at Sea* with all the sailors?

K: *Dames at Sea,* Mom. So the fact that I was in a musical called *Dames at Sea* with my boyfriend, who wore a sailor's suit, and who was better-looking than I was, wasn't a red flag?

M: I tell ya, he was better-looking than all the girls in the cast! I said to your dad, "I hate to say this, but Tom's better-looking than any girl onstage!"

K: "Better-looking than all the girls." You didn't associate that with being gay?

M: Never.

K: Didn't your generation have the term "confirmed bachelor"? When you saw someone who was good-looking, in good shape, and hadn't married, what did you think?

M: That he hadn't found the right woman, or just didn't want to be married.

TIP
IT!

K: Well, both of those things could be true. What about in the movies of your day, Mom? There was always a flamboyant sidekick in those thirties movies.

M: Well, we loved those characters. They were very funny. Like, I always heard Noël Coward was gay.

K: What?? Noël Coward was gay?

M: Ha ha, Kathy. But you see, he was so great, who cared? I didn't. All I knew was, he was funny as hell.

K: Did you ever hear that songwriter Cole Porter was gay?

M: Now see, I was shocked by that when I eventually found out, because he had a wife. He had . . . what do you call them? Ringers?

K: Ringers? You mean like a cock ring?

M: No! No, no, no. A somebody, a companion . . .

K: A beard?

M: Yes, a beard.

K: How did it go from "beard" to "ringer"? Mom, if you went into a gay sex shop and said, "Give me a ringer," believe me, they're not going to give you a single woman.

M: Anyway, as I said, we never really knew what "gay" meant. We certainly didn't think it meant they would want to marry other men . . .

K: Or flip houses in Palm Springs. So somehow, in your generation, it went from calling them "sissies," pointing and laughing in church, to hoping to God that if you buy a home, it's from a gay man. Because you wouldn't want to buy a house from a straight person, would you?

M: No. There's been a tremendous change.

As you can guess, it was really through Kathy that I got educated about gays, and only after we moved to Los Angeles from Chicago. I remember when she was performing at the Groundlings in the eighties and she'd tell me about doing a walk for AIDS. "Ma, you've got to donate something," she'd tell me.

"All right, I'll give you ten bucks," I said.

"Ten bucks! I need more than that," she said.

I gave her $25, which she was more satisfied with, but as I got to know some gays through Kathy, it became clear how much more needed to be done. It became very easy to contribute whenever I could, especially as Kathy started to do more benefits for their causes.

I've Never Seen Costumes Like That in My Life

KATHY: Okay, Mom, hold it. I want to give you some props here when it comes to gay awareness. Remember when I was in my twenties, and we were living in that Santa Monica apartment, and you came home once and said, "Dad and I stumbled upon the greatest thing."

MAGGIE: Oh yes. The Halloween parade on Santa Monica Boulevard in West Hollywood.

K: Yes! You said, "There were all these guys . . ." and I knew you meant "gay people."

M: Right. I said I'd never seen costumes like that in my life! They were doing skits and everything.

K: You said some were dressed as cheerleaders, and one guy was running around as Joan Crawford yelling, "No more wire hangers EVER!"

M: Of course. Johnny and I picked out a café and sat there all night and watched the show. It was very enjoyable. I had never seen anything like that before, and I've been to a lot of parades. We realized it was their way of showing they were glad to be out. Of course, they could get a little outrageous about it. A little in your face. There was always somebody as a nun.

K: Always a Baby Jane. Always a Cher.

M: If not Judy, there'd be a Liza. The leather stuff I wasn't keen on.

K: It's not like you haven't seen gay guys in assless chaps, Mom. Because you have. Certainly a different scene from the Fourth of July parades in Forest Park, Illinois. Let's face it, Mom, you actually exposed me to gay pride parades.

M: And then we went a lot after we moved to West Hollywood.

K: You lived three blocks from it.

M: We wanted to support it. Of course, after a while it got pretty crowded and raucous. It became harder to get a good seat, because they'd be taken up so early. But for a long time we went every year.

K: You and Dad went to gay bars, too. I mean, that was the neighborhood.

M: A great bar is a great bar. We'd go to any bar.

K: And your favorite was . . .

M: Rage.

K: Okay, now you see a bar called Rage, and what do you think the name signifies?

M: It could be "We've got a rage for this bar!" I never really gave it a lot of thought.

K: Were you regulars at the Mother Lode?

M: I don't think so. But you know the funniest thing Johnny and I ever did? We did it so innocently. We were looking for a book, and so we went to that one bookstore . . .

K: No!! Circus of Books?!?!?

M: When I think about that, oh my God . . .

K: Okay, now I don't need to explain Circus of Books for my gays, but for everyone else, it's so obviously a gay porn bookstore, from the neon sign to the mass of gay hustlers just standing around outside in tight jeans and smoking cigarettes. Mom, what were you thinking when you saw the male hustlers outside?

M: We didn't know they were hustlers. We just thought they were guys hanging around. But then we were hardly in the door and every book was nudes and poses and all that stuff. They were poses I'd never seen before and never want to see again.

K: Guys in missionary positions?

M: Don't say "missionary," Kathy. You're offending my religion.

K: Sorry, I didn't know I was going too far while you were in a *gay porn bookstore.*

M: Anyway, we did laugh about it. Johnny and I just looked at each other and thought, "We're not gonna find *The Catcher in the Rye* here."

K: Well, a different kind of catcher and a different kind of rye. Mom, what did the guy behind the register do when he saw you and Dad come in?

M: He kind of looked like, "What are they doing here?" We actually laughed about it.

K: Do you think he thought you wanted to swing?

M: Probably.

K: Were you each other's ringers?

M: Maybe so!

K: So he was probably disappointed that he lost your business.

M: Oh God, so after we were laughing, we thought, "Uh-oh, what if, as we're walking out, our friends drive by and see us?" They'd wonder what in the world Margie and John are doing!

K: Whoa, whoa, stop for one second. In a million years, what were the chances that the remaining friends of yours that were even living were going to drive down Santa Monica Boulevard past Circus of Books with its throngs of male prostitutes, on the way to church, and say, "Hey, there's John and Maggie Griffin!"?

M: Kathy, it could have happened. Anyway, we've been to other gay bookstores. Another neighbor we had, John Morgan Wilson, had a book coming out, and we went to a reading he gave at another one . . .

K: A Different Light?

M: That might have been it. Anyway, that was really nice. Swellest guy you'd ever want to know.

K: Don't swear, Mom. "Swellest guy." If that's not gay, I don't know what is.

As I got to know more gays, I got to see how different many of them are. If you watch Kathy's show, you might remember the contest she held in which the prize was for someone to come live at Kathy's house with her for a weekend. He'd get to see her perform, get wined and dined and shown Hollywood, and be treated like an honored guest. Now, the gays I'd gotten to know were pretty savvy about everything Hollywood. Some of them were so up-to-date with what's going on, they'd know more gossip than Kathy did! That's pretty hard to imagine. But at the very least, gays know about people like Bette Davis and all the old stars, but they also know the real young hot new stars! Even a gay who lives in Peoria!

Well, this one young gay who won the contest was from Cleveland, and it was funny, he didn't know anything about Hollywood! He literally knew nothing about that kind of lively gay style, or gay anything. I think it was very frustrating for Kathy. So I said, "All I know is the difference between a Cleveland gay and a California gay? Worlds apart!"

No one can say all gays are the same, I guess!

Me with those lovely lesbians Ellen DeGeneres and Portia de Rossi.

Take lesbians. I don't know much about lesbians, but don't you think it's kind of a shame we always assume lesbians are kind of husky and mannish-looking? Maybe that's because that's what they're shown as on television. But there are a lot of beautiful lesbians, too! Of course, when people see a couple of girls out together, nobody assumes they're lesbians. Straight girls are famous for living together, going out to eat together, seeing movies together, shopping. They even call each other girlfriends when they're really just friends. But when two guys are seen out together eating or at a movie, they're thought to be gay. And I don't think it's right to assume that. Even if they are gay! [*Like when Ryan Seacrest goes out to dinner with Clay Aiken. It's wrong for people to assume anything.*]

But what I really don't think is right is the discrimination and prejudice that gays still encounter. It's shameful. And the nasty things people do, beating them up and stuff like that. People who do that are cowards, real jerks.

These guys and women who are brave enough to come out, I give 'em a lot of credit. A lot of gays who recognize me on the street and start talking to me will tell me that their parents have disowned them. That's so sad. Usually it's the dads. Fathers are apparently more upset, and the mothers come around most of the time, I hear. That's why I was so excited to be with Kathy last year as a part of the West Hollywood rally against the gay marriage ban Proposition 8, which you might have seen because it was covered on Kathy's show. I went even though I really don't like to be in big crowds. But I got to be in a wheelchair at least—I don't know how Kathy walked as much as she did. [*God knows I wasn't the only one in four-inch heels that day.*]

Then, when I saw everyone with signs, I wanted one, too! So I got one to hold in the wheelchair that said GAY MARRIAGE, I'LL DRINK TO THAT! I thought that was funny.

But I was there because I had something to say as a parent. We got up onstage and I told the crowd I wanted to encourage parents to stick up for their gay kids when they come out, and that them wanting to get married is a wonderful thing.

Because when I hear these sad stories from gay sons and daughters, I think the parents are the ones who lose out when they shun their own kids.

I could never cut off a kid. It would be *my* loss.

It's got to be hard, but at the same time, what these young men and women are doing by coming out is also wonderful. I look at that "don't ask, don't tell" policy in the military and I think it's nuts. I know there's a lot of prejudice still, and I don't think gays would go after straight guys in a military situation, but a good soldier is a good soldier. [*And a naughty soldier is even better.*] What the hell's the difference?

That's why it's so great that the gays have come along like they have, establishing their own places, raising kids, and doing such a nice job at it. I think gay marriage is going to happen. It might take a little longer than the gays want, and it'll be a fight, but that's just because it's a totally different concept for a lot of people—especially from my generation—and it'll be hard for them to accept at first.

I've been asked how I can reconcile fighting for gay marriage when I was raised a traditional Catholic. Well, on one level, it's pretty simple. We never talked about gays then! You were taught to be a good parent, to be a good wife or husband, not to cheat. Good things, you know? We knew this other gay couple in our condo building, each of the men had been married before and had kids. Then they came out, because they had to do the natural thing, and now the kids they'd had from their marriages were in high school. Well, when you'd talk with them, they'd discuss their worries about the kids getting with the wrong crowd, or into drugs, how they wanted their male kid—who's straight—to meet a nice girl, and not one of these flibbertigibbets [*read: whores*], and how they wanted to put their kids through college and how expensive it was, but it was the right thing to do. And I listened and thought, "Gee, I feel like I'm talking to regular parents." The same concerns, the same worries we all have.

Anybody who's a good parent, I'm all for.

Kids have been damaged enough by all the divorce and cheating and stuff that goes on. Maybe it'll be a lot better for them if gays get to marry. Being new at it, just being allowed to do it, gays and lesbians might treasure it a lot more, because it's something they will have fought for. They'll be on their best behavior, probably!

I still have friends who wonder why I feel this way. I don't try to convince them, really. I know some wouldn't mind it, if it wasn't called marriage. A union, maybe. Nobody bats an eye at "He's my partner" or "I'm her partner" anymore. But see, the words are different. And a lot of gays won't accept that, because it makes them different once again. But don't try to convince me we shouldn't have gay marriage because straight ones are automatically better. Not with the amount of divorces I see.

Younger people accept the idea of gay marriage more, I notice. And that's where it'll have to be won. It may sound morbid, but it will be a lot better when our generation dies off!

So keep tipping it, gays and lesbians!

OLDE–TYME GAYS VS.
MODERN GAYS

Now that I think of it, when we were growing up, gay people existed. They were around, but we just thought they were more colorful than other people. I love my modern gays but things were much different back in my day . . .

Olde-Tyme Gays	Modern Gays
Much nicer mustaches, carefully groomed and often waxed into fanciful shapes	Don't really wear mustaches at all, or just have a carefully maintained coat of stubble, which looks kinda dirty if you ask me.
Used to wear bright colors like pink and purple and often had gorgeous patterns on their clothes, like paisley or a big houndstooth or even a bright gingham or checkerboard. Take Liberace, for example, that man knew how to put an outfit together. Of course, many of them always wore a neckerchief.	I miss neckerchiefs.
Gays not only wore more colorful clothes, they always got dressed up, but then again so did everyone.	I miss men wearing hats and ladies wearing dresses.

MAGGIE GRIFFIN

Olde-Tyme Gays	Modern Gays
A lot quieter about being gay, that's probably why we never knew they were gay.	Wear shirts with gay slogans printed right on the front!
Used to be married to women, and they liked it.	I'm all for marriage equality, but there are some very nice girls out there who are trying to find a husband, like that sweet Tiffany.
Used to be much funnier. We had Paul Lynde and Charles Nelson Reilly. Those two were a hoot and a half!	Now we've got that weirdo Bruce Vilanch, but at least his mom supports him.
Speaking of Bruce, gays used to all be named Bruce or Irving, so you knew they were going to be colorful fellows just by their names.	Now they have names like Mike and Robert and Dave. It's a little confusing.

TIP
IT!

MAGGIE–ISMS

[*Kathy here. If you watch* Kathy Griffin: My Life on the D-List, *you'll know that people are immediately drawn to my mom but whenever they get up close, there are a few terms she uses they aren't familiar with right away. Here, I'm providing a helpful glossary of those phrases, with my own very helpful explanations for what those terms really mean.*]

"I'LL SPEAK TO YOU FURTHER": This means the meeting is over and Maggie is done discussing the subject, at least for now . . .

"YOU COULD EAT OFF THE FLOOR": Highest praise, the ultimate sanitary compliment for a homeowner or restaurateur.

"I WOULD GIVE MY EYETEETH": Used to describe something Maggie really wants. "I would give my eyeteeth to have dinner with that handsome Bill O'Reilly."

"NEVER CARRY A BALANCE": Great financial wisdom that has kept her flush all these years, and has obviously gone unheeded by millions of people.

"DID YOU SEE THE ONE . . . ?": Used to describe a person, show, book, or movie that Maggie can't recall the name of at the moment.

"TOUGH AS NAILS": Judge Judy, who else?

"DREGS OF SOCIETY": Avoid these people at all costs, they will only drag you down.

"I ALMOST DIED!": An expression of momentary surprise, not a grave, near-fatal medical condition requiring life-saving techniques.

"GIVE THEM WHAT'S WHAT": If someone offends or wrongs someone else, this policy is put into effect.

"TEENAGERS SHOULD START OUT EVERY DAY WITH A COUPLE GOOD WHACKS, NOT FOR WHAT THEY'VE DONE, BUT FOR WHAT THEY MIGHT DO": More excellent advice. Self-explanatory.

"I CAN TAKE A SHOWER OUT OF A TEACUP": Water conservation to the nth degree.

"THEY DON'T HAVE A POT OR A WINDOW": Used to describe a situation for poor people who can't afford a convenient receptacle in which to empty their urine, or even a portal with a view, for the same purpose.

"YOU DON'T KNOW SHIT FROM SHINOLA": Used to let someone know that they are clueless and, specifically, that they can't tell the difference between excrement and shoe polish.

TIP
IT!

CHILDHOOD

*M*y kids always like to tease me about my childhood, as I described it to them.

"You always sound like you were such a goody-goody," they'll say.

Well, I was, kind of! I loved to laugh, and I loved to talk, and I never had a desire to cause any trouble. Probably because I was scared of my dad. I loved him, and he was a great, wonderful man. But you know that old saying "My father will kill me"? All of us said that in our family. Michael Corbally ran a tight ship, and you didn't want to get on his bad side! There was always my mother, Agnes, though, to thankfully see the gray where my dad saw only black and white.

She was the heart of that partnership, too, the one with the sense of humor. When you wanted something, you could go to Mom, and she'd say, "I'll go talk to the old man." Then she'd soften him up so you could get your way.

*My wonderful parents,
Agnes and Michael
Corbally, parents of sixteen!*

But when you're the youngest of sixteen, you also get the benefit of a father who's had plenty of know-how seeing what works and doesn't work in raising kids, so he'd mellowed some. By the time I came along, the neighborhood grocery store that my dad started in Chicago after he emigrated from Ireland was doing great. We were a solidly middle-class family when I got to grammar school. It was my oldest brothers and sisters who knew tougher times and who had to work in the store after school. We younger kids didn't have to when we were coming up. Of course, we were called spoiled by the older kids, and it sometimes seemed as if there were two families separated by experience and hardship, but everyone loved one another and fully supported one another through good times and bad.

I'm first-generation American. My father was a married millworker back in the old country (Ireland) until mill closings forced him to look for a better life in America. He had an aunt here who offered to sponsor his coming over, because you needed someone to help prove that you weren't going to be a drag on the economy. Not a bad idea when you think about it. So he borrowed money from his aunt to start a store, and then Mom came over with—I think, because my memory of these stories isn't the best—eight kids, including a baby no more than seven months old. Can you imagine that? She had only one niece to help her, too, and of course, they had to travel steerage, meaning they were in the bowels of the ship with hardly any privacy and little comfort. They were sick as dogs the whole way. In fact, if you've seen *Titanic,* you know how badly they were treated. And just like in that movie, some of the kids went up top to dance for the wealthier passengers, and got coins thrown at their feet. It sounds terrible, I know, but it was money.

My parents lost their first four children, two in Ireland and two in America. One died from burns because of an overturned pot of boiling water, the others to illness. The greatest number of children at any one time was twelve: Mary, Anne, Francis, Agnes, George, Pat, Angeline, Joe, John, Irene, Jimmy, and me. It meant I had quite a few siblings who felt like they could lord it over me. My oldest sib, Mary, was old enough to be my mother, and she often acted like one. I remember once on a slushy winter day heading over to see one of my girlfriends and running into Mary as she was heading home. As soon as she noticed I didn't have galoshes on she grabbed me by the coat and said, "You're not going out like that!" She dragged me home—my shoes and socks by this point were soaking wet—and I was yelling, "Leave me alone, you're not my mother!" At that age, I saw it as being bossed around. Now I think she was looking out for me when my mother couldn't.

There's one sibling I don't remember very well, Angeline. What I do remember is that she had tuberculosis, and she was in a sanitarium. She died when she was twenty-one. When I was really young, we used to go see her once or twice a week. But we could never go upstairs, because TB is so contagious, so we would wait till she came outside to the third-floor balcony and we'd talk to her from below. TB was a real concern in my day, and the Corballys didn't have great lungs, so my brother Jimmy—the next oldest—and I were always getting tested at the county hospital. Thankfully I never got it, but my sister Irene contracted it and had to drop out of high school.

I got along great with my four closest-in-age siblings: Jimmy, Irene, Johnny, and Joe. Although for a while I did hate my brother John because he used to tease me about my red hair. He had this teacher with a hideous red wig, Mrs. Burns, and he called her Wiggy Burns. Well, he called me that, too, just to get my goat. "Ooooh, I hate him!" I'd go around saying.

Interviewed about my hair. They published home addresses for the men reading!

Then he ended up being my favorite brother. He'd call me "Wig" later in life, and I just loved it. But as a kid, I was ready to kill him.

As you can guess, I wasn't too crazy about my red hair, which I got from my dad. I always used to say it was auburn, but it certainly wasn't that light, pretty red they call titian. I had freckles, too, and it just meant that when I was out, guys would yell, "Hey Red, how you doing?" Everyone thought it was pretty, but I couldn't hear it. It's true that you never like anything about yourself.

In fact, you know when I liked my red hair? When it turned gray.

My best friends growing up were my sister Irene, who was four years older than me, and Rae, an Italian girl I immediately took a liking to, who lived in our neighborhood, which was Presentation parish. Neighborhoods were really parishes then, and the name of the parish was where you said you lived. I would have said, "I'm in Presentation." Or even, "I'm in Prez." If you attended Resurrection church, you were in "Rez." St. Thomas Aquinas was just "Aquinas." Our Lady of Sorrows was just "Sorrows." Although, "I live in Sorrows" sounds kinda unhappy, doesn't it?

Anyway, Rae lived right down the street from me, and she was one of those friends you make where you click instantly. You say, "I don't know why. I just like her!"

It was evident for anyone to see, though, why the three of us enjoyed one another's company. We could see the humor in everything, and we always had one another in hysterics. Put the three of us together, and we didn't need anyone else to have a good time. In church, if somebody was singing really off-key and close to us, it would be dangerous for any of us to catch the other's eyes. Then we'd have to leave the pew to stop from laughing. Somebody with an atrocious outfit was another trigger. That wouldn't even need eye contact. Just an elbow, and an "Oh my God" was enough. Another time it was a misprint in the prayer book: "Thanks be to God" instead read "Tanks be to God."

My daughter has called it "the church giggles" in her act. Well, Irene and Rae and I could turn any situation into the church convulsions without any prodding.

Irene was particularly foxy about getting us to laugh. She could get Rae and me to make fools of ourselves, and then keep her composure while we were losing it. When she'd do this at the soda shop, they'd have to kick Rae and me out for laughing so much, while Irene got to stay! Then Rae and I would wait outside for Irene. "You always do this!" I'd say to her, still laughing, of course. [*My getting banned from talk shows is genetic. Mom was banned first, from the soda shop!*]

It's like that to this day with my best girlfriends. We're all still alive, and when any of us are on the phone with one of the others, we eventually have to hang up because it just sinks into hysterical laughter. Often over the stupidest things, stuff we've been laughing at for years. "When the three of you get together, you act like you're twelve years old!" my kids will say. But I tell ya, what good is a friendship if you can't still laugh at the same things?

Of course, when we all got married and raised children, then we'd usually be laughing about the trouble our kids were giving us! The way it would usually go is, each would defend the other's children. "Oh really, Irene, your kid's a bad one, huh? Did he stab someone?" But we always made sure never to end a conversation without a problem turning into a cause for laughter.

We also had our own secret language, which was helpful when we'd want to point out someone in the soda shop and make fun of them. [*Hmm, it seems like something else I do is genetic, as well.*] The problem was, it was all too obvious what we were doing, because we'd shift our eyes and lower our heads and speak under our breath, and it's not as if we went to a lot of trouble to disguise the words. "Looksela at that onesela with the hatsela." Or "Thatsela onesela at churchsela was a real bitchsela." My gosh, do I even need to translate it for you? [*And you want me to apologize to the people I trash? I'm now going to apologize to everyone that YOU have offended, Mom, like that poorsela bitchsela.*]

Rae's mom said it best about us. She was a sweet woman who spoke very little English—Rae, short for Raffaella, was first generation like myself—and would cook for us when we were hungry. (It's how I found out about my favorite dish, spaghetti!) Anyway, Rae's mom'd sit with us and listen to us talk, not understanding much, but knowing we were having fun. And when we'd start laughing, she'd look at us and repeat this song title that was popular then: "Cr-r-r-r-azy people!"

Laughing too much was about as bad as Margie Corbally got as a kid. I was never really rebellious, like some of my older brothers and sisters were, who reacted more strongly to my dad's strictness. See, I loved school. I liked most of my nuns. What kind of nerd was I? I loved learning, and I loved sports. I was good at learning, but not so good at sports. I was short and uncoordinated, so as much as I loved basketball and volleyball, I was always picked last, or I'd beg for the teams to take pity on me and let me play. I might not have been good, but I played my heart out!

But while I never wanted to get in trouble, I did do one

Me at twenty-one. I wish I had this thin waist again.

MAGGIE GRIFFIN

Irene, sister and dear friend, before having her large family (nine kids)!

My other dear friend Rae, with her thin waist also.

I'll only say I'm in the middle girls' row, with ugly bangs.

wrong thing in high school. Actually, it wasn't *in* high school, technically, and that's kinda the point.

I ditched one day.

I don't know what I was thinking, but these two girls convinced me to, and they were pretty daring kids. It sounded like a good idea at the time. The three of us went into downtown Chicago, saw a movie, grabbed a bite to eat, and got milkshakes. [*Maggie Griffin, the original Ferris Bueller.*] And I would have enjoyed it if I hadn't the whole time been thinking, "When I get home, if the school called my parents, I'm going to regret it for the rest of my life."

I could barely pay attention to the movie. I didn't taste any of the meal we ate. The milkshakes could have been chalk for all I knew. That Catholic guilt's a killer.

Then we got home, and nothing happened. My parents didn't know. They never found out, actually. I was safe. I realized that doing something like that wasn't for me.

But did I brag about it the next day at school?

Maybe!

MOM, MANAGER, MOMAGER

*P*eople ask me if I knew my daughter was going to be in show business, and I say, "Would you think just because your kid likes to sing Barbra Streisand songs and dance around the house that she was going to be famous?" [*It sounds like you're talking about your gay son, Mom . . . Oh.*]

As a mother, you just don't know at that stage what's in store for your child. [*Especially with an "accident baby."*] Johnny and I never took Kathy to acting lessons or singing lessons. Never even thought of it. Not that we didn't enjoy her performing for us at home. [*By performing at home, she means hovering over Hamburger Helper while I sang something from* Carousel, *and her shouting "This pah-sta's getting cold, Kathleen."*] But the idea that she'd be onstage doing it for a living was beyond our thinking. She was just this cute kid doing what cute kids do. [*Keeping us from eating our food.*] Think about it. If you

Johnny and me with Kathy. Our first Christmas in Los Angeles.

have boys, they're probably interested in sports. But do you assume they're going to play football in the big leagues one day? [*There are days I do think I missed my calling as a running back.*]

"She's sure having fun!" we'd say whenever Kathy put on little shows for us.

Did You Know You Were Crushing My Dream?

KATHY: All right, hold on, Mom. You saw my feverish attempts to entertain people. Why didn't you put me in pageants?

MAGGIE: Well, first of all, Kathy, they didn't have the elaborate ones then like you see now. So you wouldn't have liked them. You would like what's on now a lot more.

K: Excuse me, but you're reading my future mind? How does that work? Mom, I would have loved any pageant of any kind. Did you know you were crushing my dream?

M: No, I didn't, Kathy. [Rolling eyes.] I'm very sorry.

K: Thank you. I've been waiting for that apology for thirty-nine years, or whatever my real age is.

M: Add ten at least. Anyway, I'm very, very sorry about that. But . . .

K: Now, have we discussed the Sears and Roebuck charm school? I want to confront you about that.

M: Oh, okay.

K: It's something that is hurtful to me. And once again it's your fault.

M: Oh dear Lord . . .

K: When I was a student at St. Bernardine's, I believe it was about third grade, there was a speaker who came, which was always a big deal to have at assembly, because my class was only about . . . how many kids?

M: Small, twenty in a class perhaps. It was a small school.

K: So they gathered all the girls, the whole class, and we were introduced to a representative from Sears, which I believe still had the Roebuck. They offered charm school once a week, and they were going to teach us how to eat properly, behave, and walk with a book on our head.

M: Which was great. I thought it was a great idea.

K: So I then went home and told you I wanted to do it. I believe the fee was twenty dollars a class, and what did you say?

M: It was . . . I didn't have the money. It was too expensive.

K: Too expensive! Twenty dollars a week . . . to make me a *lady*. I can barely get the words out.

M: Well, Kathy, you have to understand, twenty dollars at that time was a lot of money.

K: Mother, I don't know how to walk with a book on my head *to this day*.

M: Well, I don't either, but somehow I survived.

K: Don't you get it? When you think "charm," you think Sears and Roebuck.

M: I know. That comes to my mind, first thing.

K: And you loved Sears, too. I don't get it.

TIP
IT!

M: I did love Sears. I bought all the kids' clothes there. I bought mine. I loved the catalogue.

K: Now, do you remember a certain item that we *did* get from Sears that maybe caused you a little embarrassment?

M: Oh yes I do. [Laughing] The wig.

K: If you recall, my dream was to be Barbara Hershey, who then went as Barbara Seagull because she was like a beautiful bird in touch with nature. My dream was to not be me, but to be dark-skinned with very long stick-straight hair like a Manson family member.

M: Yes, I remember.

K: Now, there was a wig in the Sears catalogue that was going to help make my dream come true. It was going to be part of my pre-op for turning into Barbara Seagull. Did you get me that wig from the catalogue, or did I get it?

M: No, no, I got it. Boy, did I get it.

K: Do you remember how much it was?

M: It was . . . I don't think it was more than ten bucks.

K: It was four. Four dollars.

M: Four dollars? Oh my gosh.

K: What I discovered was that it was called a fall, which means it would cover only part of your hair. I didn't know this.

M: Really, it was pathetic. But you thought it was beautiful. It was kind of okay from the front. But the back, there was hardly any hair . . .

K: The front was wiry red hair, and the back was long straight brown hair.

M: It was . . . look, you thought it was beautiful. Well, one Sunday, Johnny and I got up and Kathy wasn't around. We wondered, where is she? Now, in those days you didn't think too much about kids. Then you came home and walked in the door and I almost died. You had that wig on, you had put a little makeup on . . .

K: And gone to St. Bernardine's . . .

M: To the nine a.m. mass.

K: Which, by the way, was the only time I've ever volunteered to go to early mass in my life.

M: Well, I couldn't help it. You were so proud of yourself. You said, "Everybody was looking at me." I'll bet they were. I was in hysterics. I was laughing.

K: But Mother, everyone was looking at me because I was beautiful.

M: Kathy, everyone was looking at you 'cause they were saying, "What was wrong with Marge that she let her kid out like that?" Everyone who saw it thought it was hysterical.

K: Jealous. You mean jealous.

M: Of course, Johnny and I didn't want to hurt your feelings. We told you, "Oh you do look nice" and all that. But you were not going to wear that thing again.

K: Um, translation, Mom. "What the Christ were you doing wearing that in church?" You know you said that.

M: I might have. But I thought it was funny. At least I wasn't mad.

K: That is true. But would you say that's the first time I officially shamed the family?

M: Yes. That was the first time.

K: By the way, what exactly do you think our family legacy or name signifies, compared to, oh, say, the Rockefellers or the Du Ponts?

M: [Pause] Well, in our parish, we were considered kind of okay.

K: The wig didn't help?

M: The wig didn't help.

I'm guessing what probably put Kathy in mind to go into showbiz was seeing her oldest brother, Kenny, be in a band, and get a lead role in a Chicago production of the musical

Hair. Kenny used to perform every summer in a place called Saugatuck, Michigan, at a big restaurant/nightclub. It was the cutest place, like Cape Cod, and he convinced us to rent a cottage there, so we'd take Kathy and her brother John— Gary and Joyce were too old for these vacations, they were already off doing their own thing—and the kids just loved it. [*In between rolling around on the floor trying to beat the crap out of each other.*] They'd watch rehearsals, then we'd see the band perform, and it was pretty exciting for little Kathy.

One summer, when Kathy was maybe twelve, we went to a place called Nippersink Manor in Genoa City, Wisconsin, a really lovely resort that had great meals, entertainment for kids, a golf course, and a nice lake. [*Okay, the real story is that it was a place that catered to a Jewish clientele, which made Mom extra excited because she's all about the food. Let's cut the crap: that staff isn't gonna mess with a banquet hall filled with round tables of pissed-off yentas. I believe we were the only gentiles there. However, I can't confirm that the term "gentile" even exists anymore.*] The thing about Nippersink was, every so often they'd have a talent show for kids up to ages sixteen or seventeen, and we happened to be there for one of those productions. One night Johnny and I were sitting at one of the big tables where you share your meals with other guests, and the kids' talent show started. [*Kind of like a Jewish* Showtime at the Apollo. *Can I get a "what what"?*] Well, they're bringing out all these adorable children to perform, and suddenly the announcer says, "And here we have a little girl with a big voice, and she's gonna sing for you: Kathy Griffin!"

Johnny and I almost died! We looked at each other and said, "Oh my GOD!"

This was a smallish theater we were in, but boy did it suddenly seem very, very large. I started to sweat. Would she be any good? All these people from the resort are here! It's one thing to sing and act and dance for us in the house, but this was completely different. [*None of these people were having Hamburger Helper.*]

It barely registered that she was suddenly talking to us. "Hi, Mom and Dad! I'll bet you're surprised, aren't ya?" Everyone started to laugh and clap.

That's when this friendly couple next to us who we'd eaten a few meals with told us their secret. Kathy had clued them in to her little scheme. "You know, I knew and I wanted to tell ya, because I thought you should know," the lady said. "But I knew she'd be mad at me."

That sounds like Kathy. [*As Claus von Bülow would later famously say, "You have no idea."*]

Well, Kathy started to sing this Carly Simon song [*actually Roberta Flack, Mom—oh, same dif*], 'cause she was a big fan of hers, probably from sneaking into Joyce's room and playing her records. And Kathy was wonderful! You might not know this about Kathy, but she had this beautiful singing voice [*and is similar to Roberta Flack in many ways*], and she sounded great. But she was also so cute up there, all giggly and everything, not wearing a lick of makeup [*as opposed to my current signature tranny face paint*], and she waved to us as she walked off the stage. What struck me, though, was how at home she looked up there. I couldn't believe how self-assured she was when she came out to perform.

On top of that, she won an award! That was a real treat, and a big thrill for us as parents. And I'll bet that's what got Kathy to thinking she might want to do this for a living.

[*Okay, the deal was, I came in second. Not first. Second. Making me officially on the D-list at a freaking resort in Genoa City, Wisconsin. Holla!*]

Johnny and I, meanwhile, still didn't think it was anything but a hobby. We didn't take it seriously because I'd seen what Kenny had gone through with his band, making money sometimes, other times not. Real up and down, up and down. Even when Kathy pursued theater in high school and started getting leads in the shows, I still kept wondering what she was going to do with herself after she graduated. There she'd be in that real cute Jewish musical *Fiddler on the Roof,* playing the part of Hodel, the nice young daughter who angers her traditional dad by leaving the family to get married, and I'm sitting there crying, thinking that that's what Kathy would do. Little did I know, it'd be showbiz that would woo her, not a man! [*Don't worry, Mom. Plenty of busboys and barbacks would go on to screw me over in my lifetime.*]

Then again, Kathy didn't have to leave us at all to pursue her dream. In fact, we're the ones who left Chicago when Johnny decided to retire, and it was Kathy—still newly graduated from high school—who tagged along with us. You know why? Because we were headed to California, and as our oldest, Kenny, told us—because he was out there already—it's where Kathy should be. We didn't even need to ask Kathy if she wanted to move out with us. "You guys are going to California?" she told us. "Then that's where I'm going!"

Can We Get a Little More Truth in Here, Mom?

KATHY: Okay, hold it. Can we get a little more truth in here, Mom?

MAGGIE: What truth?

K: What you really wanted me to be.

M: Oh. As you got older, you mean . . .

K: Not as I got older. When I was a little girl. When you said show business was for "hoors."

M: I did not . . .

K: You wanted me to be what? Come on. You know.

M: Well, a stewardess.

K: You can't use that word, Ma. I've told you a million times. It's "flight attendant."

M: We figured if she was a stew, we could get deals on flying.

K: Do you think President Obama's mother wanted that for him when he was a child?

M: Well, whatever she wanted, he surely exceeded her expectations.

K: Thanks, Mom. So the bar was that low for me, huh? Well, go ahead, then, what was the other one? The other profession you had in mind for me.

M: A dental hygienist. For the same reason. We could go, the family could go, and probably get a little discount on checkups and cleanings. Maybe even a root canal. You know, your braces weren't cheap. I wanted to write down the amount and show you.

K: You did write it down. Like I had a running tab. How much were the goddamn braces I got when I was twelve? Were they ten thousand dollars? A hundred thousand?

M: Twelve hundred.

K: Twelve hundred? You gave me shit for ten years about twelve hundred dollars? All right. I'll let you get back to this. I just felt a little dishonesty. This idea that you were in any way supportive of my show business dreams.

M: Well, I didn't think you'd follow through on it.

K: I rest my case. I guess I know why I never got those unicycle lessons.

Look, our attitude about Kathy was, she'll do what she wants to do, and if we can help her in any way, we will. Why wouldn't we?

I think you're so blessed if you're doing something you love. I don't care if it's shoveling cement or sweeping up trash or delivering mail, if that's what you like to do. [*No one likes those jobs, Mom. No one who is actually sweeping up trash is spewing their philosophy with things like "Hey, I love what I do!"*] I don't think there's anything worse than having no interest in your work. So get a job you love! [*By the way, Mom's part-time job when I was a kid was in the cashier's office of a Catholic hospital, run by nuns that she didn't, let's just say, get along with. But remember, "Get a job you love"!!!*]

So Kathy lived with us. [*Until I was twenty-eight years old. Which I'm still ashamed of. That's way too old to live with your parents.*] And when she needed help to pay for acting classes, or those classes you take that tell you where to stand when you're on television, we supported her. She wasn't making any money at the odd jobs she had to take. You hear about these actors and actresses who say, "I came out here with two hundred dollars." What does that mean? That means the girls end up having to do nude stuff, calendars and the like. [*Let me translate Maggiespeak for you: either you're a Kelly girl temp earning money for a camera blocking class in the Valley, or you do porn.*] Makes me ill, I tell ya. I just can't see throwing a kid somewhere where they don't have a roof over their head, or a meal. And in Los Angeles, it's so much worse than anyplace else, because for every talented kid, there's a thousand behind him. For every pretty girl, there's a thousand behind her. [*Luckily I didn't have to worry about the latter category, but I fought those talented boys tooth and nail.*]

I remember once when I accompanied Johnny to a class about show business—when my husband was going out for commercials himself later in life—and at the end they asked for a donation of about ten bucks from all the attendees. Well, there was this real cute girl there, probably twenty-one, and she said, "All I have is thirty-five cents in my purse."

Johnny said, "Why don't we pay for the poor kid?"

We were too slow, because another guy stepped in and took care of her. [*I'll BET he took care of her.*] But that sure got me thinking, "My kid's never gonna go with only thirty-five cents in her purse! Never!" [*Ever since then I've had $5.35 in my purse at all times. For safety.*]

Moms and dads, if you've got a kid who wants to do this, you've got to be there for them. If that means helping them out with cash, you've got to do it.

Besides, we'd supported the other kids who went to college and paid for their tuition. This wasn't any different, to me. Kathy's acting classes, whether it was her time at the Lee Strasberg school or her classes at the Groundlings, were her college. Would I have liked Kathy to go to a regular college first? Sure, but she didn't want to do it. And to see the way she threw herself into becoming an actress when we moved to Los Angeles, how could anyone not support that desire?

TIP
IT!

Seems to have paid off, don't you think? [*Obviously here she's referring to my small supporting role in* On the Fritz, *a comedy pilot starring Los Angeles weatherman Fritz Coleman. You're damn right it paid off.*]

Giving them financial support is easy. The hard part is being with them through the disappointments. Success doesn't always come so fast in the biz. [*Mom, did you really just call it "the biz"? You old show horse.*]

Kathy would call us up and say all excitedly, "Oh Ma, I think I'm gonna get this little part in a sitcom!" Sitcom roles were a big deal. *Are* a big deal still, what am I saying? Anyway, "I'm pretty sure the part's mine!" she'd say, because the audition went really well. I'd get excited with her, which was easy to do.

Then, the inevitable follow-up call would come.

"The other girl got the part," she'd say, and then start crying. "I guess she was more the 'fresh-faced all-American' girl type than I am. I'm never gonna make it! I don't know what's wrong with me!"

Boy, is that hard to hear from your children, especially when you know how hard they're working to make their dreams come true. Well, I'd just be extra-supportive at those times, and try to get her thinking straight again. "Kathy, listen to me, the talent is there! It's got to be recognized, and it will. You have to bide your time."

In time, as we'd talk through those moments, I could hear the tears subside, and eventually she'd say, "Oh Ma, that's so great. Thanks for talking to me like that." [*Can you please become the president and chairman of all of "the biz" right now, Mom?*]

She'd get off the phone, and guess what? That's when *I'd* start crying! Now it was my husband's turn to do the consoling! "Aw geez, Johnny, is she ever gonna get a break? What's wrong with this silly town that they won't give her the part she wants? She's so talented!"

This went on for years. I didn't want Kathy to feel depressed, because she'd be so down on herself. But I would never show her that side in me. My job was to show her love and care and support, and not make it about me and my feelings.

Sometimes, as the supportive parent, you show your love by boycotting something. One of the biggest disappointments in Kathy's life, after she joined the Groundlings and started making a name for herself there in comedy, was that she was never asked to do *Saturday Night Live*. A lot of the performers from the Groundlings did go on to that famous show, and really got their careers moving along, but Kathy really wasn't for a while there. She did commercials and industrials and got little speaking parts here and there, but *SNL* didn't happen. And because of that, I never watch it. Never. Hey, I stick up for my kid!

Likewise, her dad and I would go see Kathy perform anywhere. Every week at the Groundlings, for one thing. That was a given. But then when she first started getting into stand-up comedy, we'd go to any place that would have her. And every little thing she did, we just thought it was so wonderful! If she got a little gig at a coffee shop that would let her get up onstage and tell her funny stories, we'd be there, laughing right along. She probably didn't get paid half the time at those places. [*Try fifteen years I didn't get paid.*] But at least we were now looking at our kid on a stage, and this time it wasn't us thinking, "Oh what a nice hobby she has," or wondering what career she was going to eventually get into, or whether she was going to find a man and settle down.

We could look up at Kathy and think, "She's going up that ladder!"

[*Little does she know I slept my way to the middle, and I'm proud of every rung.*]

WAYS KATHY IS SCREWING UP HER LIFE

My daughter Kathy is always getting into some kind of trouble. Here are some ways I think Kathy is ruining her life.

NAMING NAMES. Kathy can say whatever she wants, but does she have to use people's real names? Can't she use a code like "A certain blond actress," or make up a fake name, for cryin' out loud?

STRONG LANGUAGE. For Chrissake, Kathleen, watch your Goddamn mouth! Frankly, I think you embarrass that nice Anderson Cooper when you talk like that.

NOT GOING TO CHURCH. Come on, Kathy, can't you stop by once in a blue moon? Maybe every other Sunday?

ENOUGH WITH THE CRAP DIET. Would it kill you to eat more vegetables and fruit and less cake and pizza, Kathy?

KATHY DOES NOT WATCH NEARLY ENOUGH FOX NEWS. No wonder she doesn't know what the heck is going on in the world.

HOME REMODELING DISORDER. Why does Kathleen have to keep remodeling her house? It's such a beautiful house and she just refurbished it a few years ago. It's got a roof, it heats up when it's cold, and the doors lock. That should be enough.

CLOTHES SHOPPING DISORDER. Who needs that many shoes? Or jeans that come with holes in them?

I HAVE OTHER KIDS BESIDES
KATHY, PART 1

Being our first child, Kenny naturally got a lot of attention from both Johnny's family and mine. It helped also that he was a spectacularly good, happy baby.

Then we all started to notice that early on in his development, he could carry a tune. He'd sing along with whatever was being played on the radio. So Johnny took it upon himself to teach Kenny the beautiful Irish ballad "The Rose of Tralee." It was one of Johnny's favorites, and by the time he was done Kenny had learned every word, every note, every nuance to performing it.

Then, when all the relatives were over, and Kenny was running around having fun and going nuts with the kids his age, one of the adults would say, "Oh, Kenny, would you sing 'The Rose of Tralee'?"

Suddenly, as if he were some sort of little soldier, Kenny would stop, straighten up, put his hands behind his back,

My first child, Kenny,
with our first dog, Pancho.

and sing that song perfectly. There was such an innocence to it, and I'm not kidding you, he was so good people would cry.

But the minute that song was over—*bam!*—he was back to being a rambunctious little boy. That was always funny to see.

Eventually the relatives all developed a habit of giving Kenny a dollar every time he sang the song. He'd take it and put it away, or we'd keep it for him. Then Kenny got older and got into rock and roll and started his own band. Sometimes, he'd refer back to his days entertaining the family and joke about his steady compensation for his performances.

"Ma, I probably made more money as a kid singing than I do with a damn band!" he'd say, laughing.

Kenny's not with us anymore, but when I think about him, that's the memory I really cherish.

"I WANT MY MAGGIETV!"

*T*o the best of my knowledge, the Supreme Court has been whittled down to one member, and thank God it's a woman. Her name is Supreme Court Justice Judith. You may know her as Judge Judy.

I love that Judge Judy Sheindlin. She's so tiny, and cute, and sooo feisty! Tough as nails, she is, and I love it. Sometimes I think her show is the best on television. [*Just a reminder, reader: There's another show on television called* Kathy Griffin: My Life on the D-List. *In case you ever want to see the second-best show.*] It's certainly the best of all the judge shows. She gets the most respect of any of them in her courtroom. She will not stand for any nonsense, and isn't that the way a judge should operate?

"Real cases, real people," the show's announcer says. Real entertaining, I say.

When she says her trademark lines—"I didn't talk to you, don't talk to me until I talk to you" or "I'm speaking!" or "Baloney!"—I get so excited. [*Judge Kathy's version is "Suck it, court is in session."*] She talks to people like they've never been talked to before, probably, and lets us all know it's how somebody should have been talking to them all along. These are the dregs of society we're talking about. [*My whole life my mother has talked about "the dregs of society." I still don't know exactly who these people are, but I kind of think they're my peeps. I'm talking to you, cast of* Jersey Shore.]

Someone told me once that Judge Wapner from *The People's Court* griped about Judy that she was too rude, and not like how a judge should be. If I were a lawyer, that's when I'd stand up and say "Objection!" [*She makes it sound as if judges have feuds like rappers do.*]

I don't know if I could ever be a judge, though. I could never be impartial like she is. Some of these guys who appear on *Judge Judy,* they look so mean, and they look like such slobs, I couldn't give them a win if it killed me. [*"Win"? Mom really loses me when she uses that legal jargon.*] But Judge Judy sees through how they look. She may not want to find in favor of a creepy-looking guy, but she'll say, "I wish I didn't have to give you the win here, but in this case, it's the law, and I have to follow the law." You've got to admire somebody like that. [*I've never had more admiration for law-followers. They really are the earth's winners.*]

Also, even though I'm a lot older than her, we're kind of the same generation. Especially when it comes to things like dealing with computers. She doesn't get those machines, she doesn't want them, and I love that about her. [*And why did phones have to go all portable??? Grrr.*]

I think she and I would have great lunches together. She's very funny. But would I want to go up against that Judge Judy in court? Probably not! [*Mom, should I be worried? Are you involved in a conspiracy to abduct Angela Lansbury? Why are you even spending one minute worrying about your court date? I'm watching you.*]

She's great at every kind of case, really, but she's especially good where kids are concerned. She made her name in New York as a judge in family court, and boy does she get furious with parents when they pull this silly stuff where the mom won't let a dad see his own kid, or a dad isn't paying what he owes in child support. She just lays 'em low, and I get such a kick. [*You'll have to pardon my mother when she starts to use phrases from the Great War like "lays 'em low."*] At the same time, though, I can't believe some of these people can't figure out their problems together in private without going on television in front of a judge! If they had a brain cell between them, they could save tons of money and keep their kids from being so unhappy—can you imagine having to watch your parents bark at each other and air their garbage [*You mean what I do for a living, Mom? What bought your condo?*]— and it would be so much better all the way around. You can hate somebody's guts and still deal with them civilly. [*Try tell-ing that to Ryan Seacrest, Judge Maggie.*]

Then again, we wouldn't have this great television show. I tell ya, if you ever want to make your own life look like the steadiest, most rock-solid kind of life ever lived, just watch one of those judge shows.

I listen to Dr. Laura Schlessinger, too, for kind of the same reason. [*Oh Jesus, there go my gay ticket sales. Reader, you're gonna have to take it from here. The minute I saw the word "Schlessinger," which is basically the "n word" for gay people, I checked out. Good luck. I'll see you post-Schlessinger.*] She's smart, and she has a wonderful laugh, although she doesn't laugh so much anymore. Now, she's not deciding cases like Judy, but she gets tough on people who come to her with their per-sonal problems. Sometimes too tough, in my opinion. Some of these people really need to be yelled at, because they ad-mit to committing the same mistakes over and over and over again. These girls who keep going back to guys who keep beating them up, it's hard to listen to. But my mother used to say how some people should be more pitied than scorned. They're poor dumb souls, is what it is. It's kinda sad they don't smarten up, and I know Dr. Laura is hard on them be-cause she's hoping they'll eventually see the light, but I listen sometimes and go "Ooooh, come on now," and flinch. It's not the same as watching my dear Judge Judy notice a guy get-ting all sneery and cocky and thinking they can get away with smirking, and her just giving them what's what.

TIP
IT!

I could watch that every day. I certainly try to! [*Is the Laura Schlessinger part over yet? Okay good. Sorry, gays and minorities.*]

There's a lot of reality television I think is just too depressing. [*You think?*]

I can't watch too much of that show *Celebrity Rehab.* All those drug-addicted famous people acting like that, it makes you wonder why anybody would ever go on a show when you're in that condition. Making a total fool of yourself. For what? A couple hundred dollars? [*Oh, so now I have to pay Mom a couple hundred dollars? I see where this is going.*] Why would a family allow that kind of behavior to be shown? See, you've got to protect some people sometimes.

I watch shows like that, or *Jerry Springer,* and think, "Oh gee, humanity is just going downhill." I don't want that to be America! [*She wants it to be Istanbul?*]

I like *Keeping Up with the Kardashians,* though. [*Is my mom smoking crack? Is this why she should go on* Celebrity Rehab *herself?*] When I first started to watch it, I couldn't believe Kim, Khloé, and Kourtney were so uninhibited. I initially thought, "Oh, this is too much for me." Oh my God, nothing is sacred in that family! They talk about anything and everything. They're real open about sexual things, even stuff they're doing themselves! [*By "real open," I guess she's referring to Kim's sex tape. That'll make you real open real fast.*] They just don't mind that they're appearing in *Playboy,* any of that. It's like they all talk to one another and the mom like they're girlfriends.

But I developed a real fascination for them. [*Maggie Griffin, anthropologist.*] They do love the celebrity life. And you know what? They're a close-knit family. They fight a lot, and they certainly say whatever they want to one another, but they really stick up for one another against outsiders. [*By outsiders, I have to assume she means the non-Armenian community.*] So even though there's a lot of bickering, they love one another, and have a real attachment to one another. And I love that. [*Dialing Dr. Drew now.*]

Kim, especially, seems to have a lot of common sense. [*Yes. When I think Kim Kardashian, I think arbiter of common sense. "Judge Kim" can't be far behind.*] She seems to have matured a bit as she's gotten more into the business. [*Don't you mean "the biz," Mom?*] I think the paparazzi treat Kim with more respect than they do her sister Khloé, who's more upfront and says what she thinks more often. And hey, I admire Khloé for that, too. Plus, I think the mom is great. She's very pretty, and I think she's a good mom in her own way. Did you see the one when the kids bought her a pole for her birthday? I know they did it for fun, but I think the mom really uses it!

I can't imagine what I'd do if my kids got me one of those things. I just can't see me with a pole. [*Don't call my father that name.*] That really wouldn't be very interesting. But for those Kardashians? It seemed just fine.

MAGGIE'S KITCHEN

When it comes to food, hon . . . Wait, I know in these PC times, you're not supposed to call people "hon." But at a restaurant, when I want something, I can't help it. I say, "Hon, can I have a little more wine?" I know I'm not supposed to, but I'm old-fashioned. So sue me.

Anyway, back to what I was saying. When it comes to food, I like all kinds. Italian, Mexican, Polish, Chinese. [*Polish?*]

The number of foods my dad mostly ate, though, you could count on one hand: beef, potatoes, bread, cabbage, and turnips. Steak on Sunday. [*Grandpa has six fingers now, Mom.*] My mom was a good cook, but because my dad was a very basic eater, she was a pretty basic cook. He wouldn't eat turkey, pork, or chicken. Nothing green, no vegetables. If my mother wanted to make something like salmon croquettes

Me in the kitchen, stumped over a recipe. Will it turn out?

for us, he wouldn't touch that, so aside from the croquettes she'd have to make a pot roast just for him. If she made a beef stew, she'd make a separate one for us that had carrots and peas. For someone who made simple food, it could get a little complicated.

Hey look, my dad worked like a horse, and he wanted the stick-to-the-ribs meal he liked. I loved watching him eat his beloved boiled potatoes. Mom would put them in a bowl, and he'd chop them up, slather butter all over them, and then top it off with salt and pepper. It always looked so good! He lived to be ninety, so that tells you what a good eater he was. But he never changed his tune. After my mom died, I got a taste of what she had to do on the days I'd have my dad come to dinner. If it was Thanksgiving, there'd be turkey for me, Johnny, and the kids, and a little pot roast for him.

There were some things my mom made very well. She could bake a rich, hearty Irish bread with thick crust that went down so well with a lot of butter and jam on it. Add a nice cup of hot tea and you felt like you'd had a meal. Her pancakes were wonderful, too.

But when it came to trying other kinds of food, we had to go to other people's houses. My girlfriend Rae was Italian, and when I'd be over there, her mom would feed us when we were hungry. That's where I had spaghetti for the first time, and it's become my favorite dish. As my sisters and I learned about more kinds of foods, we'd occasionally say to Mom, "Can we cook tonight? Let us try something different?"

She'd say, "As long as the old man's taken care of, that's fine by me."

Then we'd set to work, making Jell-O salads, or sprucing up candied potatoes with marshmallows on top. Mom thought we were such good cooks because we were making fancier stuff. Our brothers, though, took after my dad with a lot of our experiments, and flat out wouldn't eat what we made.

When I got married, my poor husband suffered some, because Johnny's mother was a good cook. He was used to seeing different kinds of meals. So when I was learning how to put food on the table—taking tips from my mom, my sisters, and my friends—he endured his share of experiments. The great thing was, he'd never say, "Mag, this is terrible!" I might be the one complaining that something had no taste, but all Johnny would say was "Mag, don't bother to make this again." I thought that was very gallant. And I knew that was the end of that dish.

One time during the war when we were living in Spokane, Washington, in a little studio apartment in a big house, Johnny, who was in the army at that time, said he was going to bring some soldiers home for dinner. Now, these were guys who if you gave them bologna sandwiches, they'd think it was wonderful. They were just happy to be away from the base! So I was going to make the usual simple thing, spaghetti or hot dogs, but for a special treat, I thought I'd make a cake from a recipe I cut out of the newspaper. I hadn't had a lot of luck making cakes from scratch, and this was a special type of cake, so who knows what I was thinking trying something new when I was just starting out as a home cook.

Well, of course, at a certain point the older woman who ran the house we lived in said, "Gee, it should be rising by now." Oh boy, what a farce this turned out to be. The cake came out, and each layer was only a half-inch thick! It was also as heavy as a rock. Don't ask me what happened. I did everything I was supposed to do. I probably didn't have the right ingredients. I was just crestfallen. I really wanted this to be a surprise for the guys, you know? Well, this woman's grandson was there, a kid about twelve years old, and he started making fun of the cake. He kept saying, "Mrs. Griffin, you know what? You've found synthetic rubber!"

Ha ha ha. I was ready to kill that kid! [I *hear you, kid, wherever you are.*]

I got better as a cook, though. When I started having kids, I learned how to make hamburgers, pork chops, turkey, roasts. I could turn out a nice beef stew. When it came to vegetables, my kids weren't eating cabbage and turnips like I grew up with, so I had to learn how to cook carrots and green beans. I will admit for a long time I used the canned stuff, but then you get a little better, and you say, "Let me try some fresh things." That said, the children weren't really vegetable eaters. I would fix whatever and hope they'd eat it. You push the better food, of course, but kids are foxy. Hide spinach in the potatoes and they'll notice.

And if they didn't want something, they had their ways of making it look somewhat eaten, usually by pushing carrots and green beans to the edges of the plate, or scattering them around.

My cakes improved, too. I used to make lots of cakes and pies. I was a great cake maker. I made a wonderful chocolate cake with white frosting, a nice white or yellow cake with chocolate frosting. Chocolate chip cake was another of my specialties. And my lemon butter bars, which I made from scratch, were always a hit. My brownies, too.

I Did Cook!

KATHY: Whoa, whoa, whoa, Mom. Are you really trying to convince everyone that you cooked?

MAGGIE: I did cook. Who else did? You?

K: Because I'd really like to know what you thought were your best dishes. Hamburger Helper Beef Stroganoff, perhaps?

M: No, no, no, that came later, after you guys were older.

K: What, then?

M: You loved the sloppy joes.

K: That's a can of Manwich and a pound of ground beef, Mom. Don't act like you were cutting tomatoes.

M: I had my own special little touches. But it's a family secret.

K: What else?

M: Dad said I made very good Italian spaghetti for an Irish girl.

K: That's not exactly a compliment.

M: Well, what about my . . .

K: McDonald's?

M: Oh, you kids love making it sound as if McDonald's was all I ever fed you.

K: Maybe because one of your "recipes" was throwing cash at us to go down to the McDonald's. Remember? You'd come home from work . . .

M: Well, that's true . . .

K: . . . and lie down on the olive green couch and say, "Here's a dollar."

M: Occasionally that would happen. If you remember, Kathy, that was a treat for you guys. You loved it when that McDonald's opened up down the street.

K: And then everything changed. Fess up, Mom. Tell everyone about Fridays. Why it was "Thank God it's Friday" for you before there were T.G.I. Friday's.

M: On Friday nights, when I worked at the hospital, I'd wait for your dad to come home from the store, and then after I left to go to work, he and one of you kids would go down to McDonald's and he'd get their fish sandwiches for everyone.

K: What was it? The Sabbath? Is that what Friday was?

M: Oh, the fish.

K: What the hell is that fake Catholic holiday?

M: It wasn't a holiday, Kathy. It was a religious observance. On Friday you didn't eat meat.

K: But that doesn't make it appropriate or acceptable to send your children down the street for McDonald's.

M: Well, I thought it was okay. Look, when you became the last one in the house with us, I didn't want to cook much anymore. All right? You were such a pain anyway, so picky. All you'd ever eat as a kid was grilled cheese sandwiches and pizza. That was it. Honest to God . . .

K: I was vegan! Did you ever think about that? Or thanks to McDonald's, a pescatarian.

M: You did like pancakes.

K: That's why I didn't take a crap until I was fifteen, Mom. Because I ate grilled cheese sandwiches, McDonald's, and pancakes.

M: You didn't even like hamburgers.

K: Was that part of your "cooking"?

M: That's my cuisine.

K: And really, Mom, how many cakes have you ever made from scratch?

M: I'm not going to talk about that. Look, my cakes from the box were better than my scratch. But they became very good,

Me with a cake I baked myself. Take that, Kathleen!

and even my friends who would always bake from scratch went to the cake mix boxes.

Okay, when boxed cakes came along, they were great. But I learned ways to enhance them and make them better. Maybe you'd put an egg in when they didn't recommend it. Or I'd use a little more vegetable oil. Maybe if I was making a white cake, I might add orange juice to give it a little tang. With something like banana bread, I might put a little bit of applesauce in. It doesn't hurt the taste and it keeps them nice and moist. I just hate dry cake.

Of course, today I can't handle rich desserts like I used to.

Where before I might be able to eat a whole dessert, I can't anymore. I have to tone it down. [*Kirstie Alley will pick up the slack, don't worry.*] Same with some of the heavier meals I always loved, like clam sauce with spaghetti. I almost feel sick afterward. And as much as I adore Mexican food, I have to beware of the spicy dishes. I like them, but they don't like me.

It's a different world now with food than when I was growing up. For one thing, there's more access to cuisines from around the world. Salads are everywhere, and not just in summer. We never got lettuce or tomatoes or cucumbers in the winter when I was younger. Winter was cabbage and turnips. Food was truly seasonal. Now you can get strawberries and blueberries all year round. They might come from Argentina, when it's their summer and our winter, and you might pay more for them, but to get them whenever you want them is just wonderful. Plus, food has so much more flavor now. Take what people do with vegetables. In my day you put butter on vegetables. Now you might have different herbs on them, and put olive oil over them instead of butter. And hey, they're just as delicious that way! But every once in a while I'll grab that pat of butter, especially for something like baked potatoes. I should never have baked potatoes. Between the butter I put on them, the sour cream, and the chives, they're a whole meal.

Nowadays, people worry about food more. I tell ya, I would not want to be a parent today, the way young girls are concerned about their weight and figure. They're all so sylphlike now, it's disgusting. [*Which is why they're all on the covers of magazines.*] They'd look better, frankly, if they ate a baked potato or two every once in a while. See, in my time we got our vitamins from the food we ate. Whereas today, people get them from supplements, and that can't be better. I don't know what I'd do if I was a mom with a young daughter on the verge of bulimia or anorexia. It doesn't help that they all want to be Britney Spears and Paris Hilton. The fetish for thinness is a real problem.

I guess it all started when television came in. That's one way it ruined the country. [*Don't talk like that around my Emmys!*] That's when everybody started to eat in front of the television, and even after dinner. Chips and candy and everything. TV changed everybody's eating habits. You started seeing more fast food, and that's when everybody started to get fatter. We were guilty of it, too, in our household. Something good's coming on TV, and you want those snacks.

Know what my downfall is? [*Besides your love of Bill O'Reilly?*] For all the kinds of food I like, what I can't resist is chips and dip. That's been my guilty pleasure for as long as I can remember. A bag of Ruffles—'cause their chip is thicker and it doesn't fall apart—and an onion dip, or tortilla chips with a nice guacamole or salsa. Then maybe a little sweet after that.

If you listened to Kathy, she'd tell you I eat like a nineteen-year-old frat boy. Look who's talking! At least I like the food that's good for me, too! Geez.

HOW TO THROW A PARTY,
GRIFFIN STYLE

1. MAKE SURE YOU STOCK THE BAR. Nothing loosens up a party like some cocktails. A nice Tom Collins or an Old-Fashioned with an orange slice is sure to impress and a Hot Toddy or a Brandy Alexander helps make guests sleepy for when you want them to leave.

2. PUT OUT SOME CHIPS AND DIP, AND SOME CHEESE AND CRACKERS. You can't let your guests go hungry. If you're throwing a party for a special occasion, dust off the ol' Crock-Pot and whip up some tasty Swedish meatballs. I'd give you the Griffin family recipe but then everyone would be going to your party instead of mine.

3. FOR ENTERTAINMENT, MAKE SURE YOU KNOW SOMEONE WHO PLAYS PIANO. Karaoke is for duds. There's nothing like live entertainment to show folks you've got class. Or just get a kick out of your brother-in-law Maurice's profanity-laced screeds ("A couple of real goddamn nitwits here") against your politics.

4. WATCH THE DOOR TO THE BASEMENT FOR LITTLE PUNKS who want to steal valuable stuff. (See "An Open Letter to the Bastard Who Stole Our Sword," page 164.)

TIP
IT!

I'VE MET CELEBRITIES!

*A*s long as I can remember, I've loved movie stars. Television stars, too, although television came later. [*Are you sure?*]

See, I'm old enough to be able to tell you that I saw, in person, a young . . . no wait, I'll save it! [*Wow. Making us wait for it. This better be good, Maggie.*] Anyway, it was one of the biggest thrills of my life, I tell ya. Here's what happened: I was in my third year of high school—this would have been 1937—and one of my older sisters and her husband took me and Irene on a trip to Hollywood over the summer. My brother-in-law knew somebody at Metro-Goldwyn-Mayer [*which to us Griffins was synonymous with "I know someone from Mars"*], the biggest studio of the day, and with that connection we got passes to go on the lot.

I couldn't believe it, we were just roaming around where they made the movies I loved so much! Well, who should come out of nowhere, it seemed, but a pretty young girl skipping along the sidewalk. It was Judy Garland! [*I'll bet she was "skipping."*] We stepped aside so she could go by, and Irene and I didn't say anything because we were too nervous. But we really wanted to say hello. She was so adorable-looking! Her hair was very reddish; I thought it would be more brown. She had makeup on, too, which I guess was for whatever movie she was filming. Once we caught our breath, we thought maybe we'd have a chance to say hello to her, so we ran to try to catch up to her—hoping maybe she'd slow down—but right at the moment we were close enough she turned into an office. [*She probably thought she was running for her life. That's what "the dolls" will do to ya.*]

Boy, I wish we could have said something! It's a big regret of mine. She seemed like a nice, innocent girl, just like me. [*Like when I see Angelina Jolie on the street, and I think, "She's just like me."*] She and I were nearly the same age. But I'll bet she was a lot more grown up than I realized.

I got to actually meet one of my favorites—the beautiful Lana Turner, another MGM star—when she came to the army base in Spokane, Washington, where my husband, Johnny, was stationed during World War II. The stars would often come to the bases to entertain the guys—like Kathy did in Iraq and Afghanistan [*me telling pussy jokes in the desert is very different, I just want to make that clear*]—so when Lana came, Johnny said I could come to the base to see her. Well, she came out, stood onstage [*and told pussy jokes?*], and then talked to all the guys, who were just going nuts, clapping and everything. She hung around for pictures and autographs, and then it was time to leave. Her car was there ready to take her away. I was nearby and I said out loud, "Oh darn, I'd love to see her up real close [and judge her] and say hello or something."

Well, her agent was right there, and he turned to me and said, "Come on! You want to meet her?"

Now, you say these things sometimes, then when you get your wish, wouldn't you know it, you get cold feet. Like I did just then. [Oh Christ.]

Suddenly the prospect of actually meeting her seemed too bold. And she was only ten feet away at the most! But see, she was already in her car with her mother. The agent opened the door and said, "This lady would like to say hello."

"Oh hi, how are you?" I somehow got out. I didn't know what to say. I probably called her "Lana," as if I knew her or something! Oh geez . . .

Her people were very nice, and then the agent said, "Lana, come on, how about taking a picture with her?"

Now I was appalled. I thought, that's so terrible to ask her to get out when she's already seated in her car, ready to leave! "No, no," I said. "I just wanted to say hello!"

"No, come on. She'll take a picture."

"Honestly, this is fine. Thank you."

I backed away, the agent gave up, and then she was gone. Readers, I have never been so sorry that I didn't get that picture. I would give anything to be able to go back and redo that moment. But I'll be honest with you. You know why I really backed down? I wasn't sure I wanted to stand next to such a pretty star.

Vanity will get you every time.

"We All Went and Stalked Celebrities"

KATHY: Ugh. Mom. Depressing. So your life is a case of missed opportunities . . .

MAGGIE: I know.

K: And feeling inferior to others.

M: Now, I did once refuse a picture with Clint Eastwood.

K: Okay, now you're just making shit up.

M: No, no, at the golf tournament. I have pictures of stars from that. But Clint was taking pictures with a lot of the girls there . . .

K: Probably hot twenty-year-olds. Then you and Dad showed up with golf bags.

M: He came over and said, "How about if I take a picture with you?"

K: You are making this up.

M: I said, "No." I said, "I'll tell you what, my husband will take a picture of you alone, and that will be nice."

K: Okay. Are you going to tell the Johnny Carson story? Because your Clint moment sounds a lot like that one.

M: Well, let's see, we were living in Santa Monica, right across from the Civic Auditorium. And I wanted to walk into downtown.

K: Mom, get to the point.

M: All right, all right. Anyway, the stars were giving a big benefit there.

K: And how did you hear about it? Did you get an invitation in the mail? Come on . . .

M: Well, I saw it in the paper.

K: And? What did you do? You . . .

M: Well, I . . .

K: You dressed us all up and we all went and stalked celebrities. Why won't you admit this? When we first moved to California, you would read in the paper or the trades about where celebrities were, what ProAm tournaments or what gala benefits they were going to be at, and you would go and pretend you were attending. And you would stalk celebrities.

M: We didn't bother them or anything, Kath. We were respectful. Anyway, I saw all the limos at the Civic Auditorium, and I decided I'd see if I could go into town that way . . .

K: Illegal. Not appropriate.

M: . . . to see if I could maybe see somebody . . .

K: No badge. No pass.

M: . . . and nobody stopped me! So anyway, I went over there, and I'm near the stage door, and it was great. I saw Rosie Clooney come in, Sammy Davis Jr. . . .

K: Again, were you invited to this event?

M: No, of course not. This was earlier in the day. It was their practice. They didn't care. I was the only one there, anyway.

K: It's kind of amazing you haven't served hard time.

M: Anyway, Johnny Carson comes out, and he was smoking. He wanted a cigarette, I guess. He was standing maybe ten feet away!

K: I'm sure the restraining order said fifty feet, but whatever.

M: I saw him.

K: Stared at him with a camera, more likely.

M: I didn't have a camera.

TIP
IT!

K: But you had that trench coat, and that look. That look!

M: I didn't take a picture. I took one with my eyes. I was kind of dying to say "Hi!" I would have called him Mr. Carson, too. But see, I knew he was shy, and that he hated parties and people talking to him.

K: Ma, you weren't at a party. You had broken into a celebrity event you weren't invited to. It's not as if you were "partying" with Johnny Carson.

M: Anyway, he just finished his cigarette, and he was uncomfortable, I could tell. I was uncomfortable, too. I kept looking the other way, pretending I was waiting for someone.

K: Mom, this sounds like you're ex-lovers.

M: I kept looking at my watch, you know how you do. I didn't really want to walk away then, but I did. He was enjoying his moment of solitude.

K: Okay, Mom. Let me stop you, because this is *never* how I heard this story. This is how I heard it. You saw Johnny Carson, who seemed "high and mighty," like he wanted to get recognized, and you *weren't going to give him the satisfaction.*

M: Well, I might have . . .

K: And for years, Dad would tease you and say, "Oh Mag, how devastated Johnny Carson would be because you wouldn't give him the satisfaction of recognizing him." I'll bet that was the case with Clint Eastwood, too.

M: Well, that's probably the truth. Look, I really was uncomfortable.

K: Do you think that changes your lies?

M: Oh, don't you have something better to do?

Although Kathy would like everyone to think we were stalkers, we weren't. We just liked to go places where celebrities were, and when we moved to Los Angeles, there were so many places like that!

For one thing, if you drive around, you just might see the big trucks that indicate filming is going on. Johnny and I might be headed somewhere in our car and notice the trucks, so we'd pull over and get out and try to see what was being filmed. One time it was an Andy Garcia and Richard Gere movie, and they were just using somebody's real house to film. We hung around waiting for something to happen, and then suddenly the production called it quits for a while, and before you knew it they were standing around a few feet from us! We just walked by, didn't talk to them or ask for pictures or anything, and that was pretty exciting. It's probably a little harder to do that now. You see a lot more cordoned-off sections.

I never asked for autographs. I don't like that. What the hell am I gonna do with an autograph? Not interested, don't collect them. I'd much rather get a picture. Darn it, why didn't I get that nice Lana Turner's?

It's tricky figuring out when to approach a celebrity and when not to. When Johnny and I would go to the golf tournaments every year [*that they were not invited to*], there was designated time for the stars to pose with you and give autographs. [*A system designed to gently appease the John and Maggie Griffins of the world.*] But you weren't supposed to bother them while they were golfing. My husband, being a golfer, understood that and would never have done that in a million years. But if they were walking from tee to tee, they'd get approached. But we never did that. We always waited till they were finished. [*Or you decided they were finished.*] Of course, someone like Jack Lemmon, who always comes across so friendly on television, was never that friendly taking pictures at the golf tournament. [*Kind of like the way I get really pissed at Roger Federer during U.S. Open matches when he never turns and waves at me. What a dick.*] He loved golf too much, and I think he was always worried about how he was playing. As for why I didn't get a photo with Clint Eastwood at that one tournament, I guess I just wasn't a fan. [*I hear from Camp Eastwood that this devastating news will be impossible for him to recover from. Stay strong, Clint.*] We got Telly Savalas's though. Johnny and I loved his TV show, *Kojak*. I know, I know. Which would I like to have more now? But in those situations, you go with who you like. [*Did you really see a subtle dig at Telly Savalas coming? I didn't.*]

A great place to see stars is the Beverly Hilton hotel, because a lot of the big events and awards shows happen there, like the Golden Globes and the AFI Life Achievement Awards. Johnny and I loved to go there and hang around the lobby [*aka loitering, which I believe is a misdemeanor*], maybe get a drink in their nice bar, and wait until we could see somebody. [*Or see at all, depending on how much they'd been drinking.*] Since they had to come out to go to the bathroom, we'd often catch a glance at them that way. It's a nice way to see celebrities because they're all dressed up, looking their best. I saw Princess Grace once, and I nearly fainted. [*Oh Jesus, please don't tell me I'm going to learn that my mother followed Princess Grace into the john.*]

One night we were there—I forget the occasion [*that we weren't invited to*]—but there was a break between the dinner part and the ceremonies part [*and clearly a break in security*], so Johnny, Kathy, and I decided to step out for some fresh air. [*Oh crap. I'm an accomplice. I admit it. I was there. And it was frickin' awesome.*] It was a really beautiful summer night, I recall. Well, who should be stepping out for a stroll, too, but Gene Kelly and his wife! They must have wanted a cigarette break, because they were walking and smoking. We didn't have a camera with us, but Kathy did, so she went up to this great musical star and said, "Mr. Kelly, can I take a picture of you?" [*I'm such an asshole. Why couldn't I leave poor Gene Kelly alone?*]

He said, "You can take it, but we're not gonna stop walking."

I thought that was fine. Not snotty at all. Kind of like a compromise. He wasn't going to stop us from taking the picture we wanted, but he wasn't going to take any extra measure to make it easy for us because he wanted a nice walk with his wife. Kathy had to walk backwards to get it, but she did. I wish I knew where that photo was now. [*Phew. That would have been some embarrassing shit for me.*]

Johnny and I saw Gene Kelly and his wife again when we ate dinner at a favorite restaurant of ours, called Scandia. We didn't like the table they sat us at, so we requested a different one, and it turned out to be right across from you know who! Of course, we were dyin' to look at them, so you have to figure out how to be casual and eat and not think about the fact that one of the biggest movie stars ever is right next to you! But see, we would never have bothered them in that situation. They're trying to have a meal, after all. I think they had pasta. We did, too! [*Going unsaid here is that my mother obviously wanted the table closest to the bathroom, making it easier to trap unsuspecting A-listers into a photo. Even Clint Eastwood has to take a piss.*]

Another great place to see stars is at a Screen Actors Guild strike. Kathy got in SAG early because of a commercial she made as a teenager in Chicago, so when she joined the picket line, we got lots of nice pictures. The actors' strike was even better than the golf tournaments, because whereas the golf event attracted mostly guys, the strike gave you the guys and the girls! [*It's like going to the slaughterhouse and saying, "Those calves were adorable!" I don't really think the purpose of a union strike . . . oh never mind.*]

We had a near disaster with Elliott Gould when we saw him at the strike and wanted a picture with him. He was really big at the time [*ouch*], and some young kids who wanted his picture, too, were getting a little pushy about it. They're very bold sometimes, these teenagers, and they'll just go right up and say things to a celebrity. Well, this one kid was doing just that, insisting on an autograph, and Elliott barked back, "No, I don't want any pictures!"

Gee, thanks, little brats, for ruining it for everybody! [*Why do I think those "teenagers" were named John and Maggie Griffin?*]

Well, I had an idea. I said to Johnny, "You know what I'm going to do? I'll go over and get near him, but stay behind him. Then, see if you can get the two of us together." [*News flash: My mother was the first photobomber. You just got schooled, Harvey Levin.*]

Here I am, a woman in her early sixties, trying to sneak a photograph with a star! I went over and stood real quietly, and there's Johnny trying to get into position to take the picture. I'm all relaxed and smiling for my husband, and then Elliott turned around to look at me. He must have noticed Johnny and the camera. I knew he was going to say, "Hey, what's goin' on?"

TIP
IT!

But instead, he smiled and said, "What are you doing back there? Come on and get up with me. I'd love to have my picture with you!"

I almost died. What a nice man! [*The woman really knows how to play the age card, doesn't she? She played that poor Elliott Gould like a fiddle.*]

We got a nice picture of Jack Nicholson, too, although I nearly got knocked to the ground for it. [*When you play the game hard, Mom, sometimes there are casualties.*] I guess I didn't recognize him standing near me, because he had a cap on. But before I knew it, at least seven photographers got into a real fit and rushed him, pushing so hard I fell right into him. I thought, "Who is this guy?" Then I saw the smile, that sneaky smile. No wonder, I realized. My big meeting with Jack, and it could have broken my hip! [*You should see the other guy.*] I'm glad Johnny was there to get the picture. Those paparazzi, they can be terrible when you're trying to get a snapshot of somebody famous.

Once Kathy became successful, though, I got to meet all kinds of celebrities through her, and that's just been wonderful. She would take Johnny and me to film sets, TV shoots, awards shows, and the like. It was really fun for us, and it continues to be fun for me. Who would have thought all those years ago, watching stars on television like Milton Berle, Dick Cavett, Liza Minnelli, and Carol Burnett, that years later chatty Kathy from Forest Park, Illinois, would be performing with them!

Left:
Loni Anderson with her fofties. Johnny probably took this one.

Middle:
Elliott Gould at the actors' strike. He didn't like these obnoxious kids.

Below, left:
I almost got trampled when Jack Nicholson showed up!

Below:
Jack Lemmon wanted a smoke, and we got a snapshot!

Or that we'd get to see them up close and get to say hi! Kathy talks so easily with them, but when I get around a star, I may think I'm very relaxed and casual, but that's clearly not the case. When we met cooking star Paula Deen for dinner, who I just love, I kept saying, "Well, Paula Deen says this" or "Paula Deen says that." Kathy finally said, "Ma, Paula Deen is right there. You don't have to say her last name all the time!" Everybody laughed, but that's just the way I am. [*Crazy?*]

Don Rickles, for instance. Meeting Don was an ultimate favorite. Friends of mine over the years have taken offense at the jokes he's made, but I think he's great. Nobody ever really got mad at Don, because there was never any meanness to him. That's why I don't want Kathy to get mean-spirited. Like with Ryan Seacrest. She just loves to pick on him, you know? [*Pick on "her," Mom. "Her."*]

Anyway, the day I met Don, it was a big secret I wasn't to know about, apparently. I knew they had made an appearance together at the Emmys. Kathy helped him out onstage and got the crowd to stand up and cheer for him. I was so proud of her. I thought, "Kathy, now that's class!" That showed a good up-bringing, because this man who's been so big for so long deserved that reception. Well, all I knew was I had to go over to Kathy's house, and that the *D-List* cameras would be there. The only hint I got was that the producers kept saying, "Somebody's coming over that we think you'll like." Believe it or not, I had no idea.

When I got there, they had me wait a bit, and then they told me to go upstairs and into the kitchen, because that's where they said this mystery guest was. When I got there to the table, everybody was blocking this supposedly special guest. Then tour manager Tom and Kathy's assistant Tiffany pulled away, and Don Rickles was sitting there.

I almost died!

Why don't they ever tell me in advance? Thank God I was wearing something decent and my hair looked good! [*As opposed to naked and bald?*] Well, he was just so delightful and so sweet. And what else? Funny! He kept up the quips, I'm telling you. He said that when Kathy told him he was going to meet her octogenarian mother, he expected to see somebody shuffling in with drool hanging out and terrible hair.

Laughing, I said, "I think I look like the person you're talking about."

"Aw," he said, "you're beautiful! You're beautiful!"

That's how cute he was. Everybody was in love with him. He was funny on camera, naturally, but off-camera is when he gets serious. He asked me how long I'd been married, and when I told him nearly sixty-five years, he said, "That's great!" Because his record is good, too. Over forty years with his wife, Barbara!

Then I said, "I think it's so wonderful that you and Bob Newhart and your wives have been such great friends."

TIP
IT!

101

Me with the great Don Rickles, a sweet, classy, hilarious guy.

He zinged back with, "You had to ruin the conversation, bringing that jerk's name up! And we were having such a great time!"

I know guys hate it when you say they're sweet, but that Don Rickles, he really was lovely. [*So true, Mom.*]

I CAN LIVE OUT OF MY PURSE
(AND YOU CAN TOO, AS LONG AS YOU ALWAYS CARRY THESE ITEMS)

1. TISSUES. I don't give a hoot what Kathy says, everyone needs a tissue at least once a day.

2. MLV MAKEUP KIT. Remember all you need is mascara, lipstick, and Vaseline to look sharp and lovely.

3. COUGH DROPS. Good for coughs but also handy if you've got a dry mouth or a sweet tooth.

4. ANOTHER PURSE OR TWO. I can live out of my purse, but you should have an extra in case you need to downsize.

5. RUBBER BANDS. The greatest invention since the wheel and sliced bread.

6. YOUR TEETH. Enough said.

7. SCRAP PAPER. It's always good to have something to write on if you need to send out a VIP (Very Important Paper)!!!

8. HAMBURGER HELPER, or a bread roll you squirreled away from a restaurant. What if someone gets hungry?

9. A PHOTO OF YOUR FAVORITE DREAMBOAT. Mine's Robert Young, but pick whoever you like.

10. A CAMERA, in case your favorite movie star walks by at the fancy gala you're standing outside of!

11. YOUR ID. When you're a senior like me, it comes in handy for free meals and discounts at the golf course, the movies, and national parks. I call it my senior card.

12. PAPER TOWELS. They clean up any mess a tissue can't handle.

MAGGIE'S GUIDE TO
L.A. HOTSPOTS

Pavilions

I love my Pavilions supermarket in West Hollywood. [*Wait.
She's not really going to write an entire Hollywood highlights section
about a supermarket, is she?*]

First, though, you should know that it took a while for me
to love supermarkets. My dad had a neighborhood grocery
store, and because of that, we hardly ever traded at the A&P,
which was the big grocery when I was growing up. The A&P
was competition for my dad. [*Who says "traded" anymore? Was
wampum involved?*]

"They'll kill me on price," Dad would always say. "I can't
begin to sell stuff as cheap as they do." [*Why didn't he just
outsource it to India?*]

But at least my dad was smart. Wherever he had a store,
it was in a neighborhood where citizens might find it

inconvenient to go out to the chains. [*That is a great name for a gay bar, though. Meet me at The Chains!*] People didn't always have cars then, so they relied on their local store. But as I got older, and started a family, stores got bigger, and you started seeing more supermarkets. I always tried to shop at a family-run place—if not my dad's, which he worked at till he retired—but when we moved out to California, the Safeway was a couple of blocks away from our first place, and I loved it. They had everything. Meat, fish, even makeup. Corner stores just didn't have that variety.

Then we moved to West Hollywood, and the Pavilions worked out beautifully. They recently remodeled it, too, and now they have a great deli, you can get pizza, sushi (although I don't eat sushi) [*Who would? That foreign shit'll kill ya*], and a Starbucks coffee! [*So much for the mom-and-pop song and dance.*] There's even a little outdoor eating place, so you can sit down there [*and judge others*] instead of going to the bar or the coffee shop. It was time for them to remodel, too. It was getting a little rundown, and in a gay area, that's just not tolerated. [*Preach!*] The Ralphs supermarket nearby had already remodeled, and it was much nicer. Pavilions almost lost me to Ralphs.

Of course, I knew where everything was at the old Pavilions. I could shop fast. The new one, I don't always remember where the canned soups are. Let's put it this way, I get in a good walk when I go to the new Pavilions, whether I want one or not. Also, everyone's [*read: gay men are*] real nice if they recognize me and want to say hi [*read: "Hey gurl!"*] and get a picture. But I'm usually very serious when I shop. I'm not looking around to see who's noticing me, and I'm certainly not dressed up to get noticed. One time, though, this lady [*named Henry*] came up to me, and she was very nice, but as God is my judge, she followed me for the rest of my shopping.

I'd pick out my milk, then she'd be right next to me. "Have you tried this brand?"

I'd pick out my oranges. "Oh, these oranges are better than the ones you picked."

I'm so chicken, I took the ones she chose, just to be accommodating. But I wanted to say, "Gee, lady, we talked already for a while. Can I get my shopping done and get outta here?" [*Who's Sean Penn now?*]

If I don't learn that new Pavilions fast, that could be a problem.

Rage [*Not "anger," readers; Rage, the gay bar in West Hollywood*]

One day Johnny and I were walking home to our apartment in West Hollywood, and he said, "Gee, Mag, it's still so nice out, why don't we have dinner out instead of at home?"

"Sounds great!" I said.

Well, we happened to notice this cute little terrace area on Santa Monica Boulevard, so we went in and asked if we could sit there. They couldn't have been nicer to us. It was four thirty in the afternoon and only a few other tables were taken, so the bartender killed himself to give us this lovely spot. [*He didn't really kill himself.*] We noticed it was happy hour [*Ah, "dinner"*], so we got potato skins and chicken kebabs, and they were the best hors d'oeuvres we'd ever had! Plus, the wine was only $4 a glass! We *might* have even ordered a third glass to share.

I tell ya, we sat there for two hours, and it was wonderful. We saw that there was music playing and dancing going on [*Btw, it's clearly nine p.m. at this point*], but we had a nice view of the outside, so we didn't pay any attention. Well, we went back a couple of weeks later, and again, they couldn't have been sweeter. The food was just as good, too. We even got a free cup of coffee. This was looking to be a regular place for us!

A short while after our second time there, our nice gay neighbors Randy and Steve were visiting, and one of us happened to mention, "Gee, we stopped at Rage the other night."

It was hardly out of our mouths when they both said, "WHAT? You guys went to Rage?"

"Sure, why?" Had we done something wrong?

"Um, did you look at the video screens? Did you see what was going on inside?" [*In other words, select clips from* Jurassic Prick *and* Who Rimmed Roger Rabbit.]

I told them we were there at four thirty in the afternoon! What would be going on then? That's when I found out that

Rage is a gay bar. Well, every bar in that area is gay, but you know what I mean. I guess it would have been a different scene if we'd started our happy hour at eight p.m. And I have to assume the people there were glad we wanted to face away from the inside!

Randy and Steve got a big bang out of that. [*I think Randy and Steve have had quite a few big bangs.*] Really, every gay guy who heard was in hysterics, too. Of course, when we mentioned it to Kathy, she had a similar response.

"You went to RAGE?" she said. "Talk about *me* shaming *you!*"

McGinty's Irish Pub

My brother Pat had a tavern in Chicago [*Hold on a second, are you implying that Irish people from Chicago have bars? Unheard of!*] that we loved going to, so when we moved to L.A. Johnny and I did our best to find a similar one.

Well, bless the day we found McGinty's in Santa Monica! [*That's what church is for!*]

We loved going there. It wasn't fancy, and sometimes you'd look around and think, "Would it kill them to paint the place once in a while?" But it was clean—if a little cruddy-looking— and Johnny loved all the Irish beers and stouts they had. Now, Irish taverns aren't the same as English pubs. The English like a nice fireplace, comfortable chairs, attractive furnishings. The

Irish have a saying: "If you want comfort, go home." [*The Irish have another saying: "Move out of your mother's house, you drunken forty-year-old."*] Don't get me wrong. I love the English, I love their accents—although I'm not so keen on that Cockney slang, since I can't understand it—and their pubs are so quaint and cute. But the Irish don't go for that quaintness.

McGinty's was like a real nice neighborhood place, and there was a strong Irish clientele. You'd hear names of towns and counties in Ireland as you sat at the long communal tables. You could play darts, and they had great food. They even had Indian cuisine, because of the connection to England, I guess. Johnny didn't really care for Indian food. But they had great potato dishes and sandwiches.

I don't think it's there anymore, though. It might be called something else. [*Ma, you could have said this up front. I was really looking forward to some Indian potatoes.*]

You'll probably have to go to Tom Bergin's or Molly Malone's instead. They're okay. Or the Cat & Fiddle in Hollywood. You can sit outdoors there, and they have a nice fountain. Great mac and cheese.

The Penmar Golf Course

Johnny and I were big golfers, and this was our favorite course in L.A. It's by the Santa Monica airport, it's reasonably priced—they have senior rates!—and it's perfect for beginners because the courses are kind of flat; it's mostly par threes and par fours. (And all you ladies, one of the holes is par four for men, but par five for us!) Plus, it's a nine-hole course, so you don't take up too much of your day in case you wanted to get other stuff done, or maybe catch a happy hour across town. They have a coffee shop, too, in case you get hungry. The key is that everyone's friendly there. We made some great pals at Penmar, like Skip Belden. Hi, Skip!

The Polo Lounge at the Beverly Hills Hotel

Johnny and I would go to the Polo Lounge all the time and sit in their lovely garden area. You'd always see a celebrity! [*Please sweet Jesus, let it be Robert Young, dead or alive!*]

We'd take all our Chicago friends there when they came to visit, and it didn't disappoint as a place that makes you feel like you're in Movieland. So if you've got friends in Los Angeles and you're out for a vacation, get them to take you there for happy hour—you never know who might be stopping by after work on a TV show or movie shoot! Don't make a habit of it, though. It can be expensive.

I HAVE OTHER KIDS BESIDES KATHY, PART 2

*W*hen Joyce was born, she was the only girl on Johnny's side of the family for a long time—all boys among the grandkids, I tell ya—so she got a lot of favored treatment. You'd have thought she was a princess, the way she was doted on, and I'm not saying little Joyce didn't enjoy it. Who wouldn't?

But she didn't let that define who she was. Joyce really got into books and reading, and since we had a library right down the street from our house, smart little Joyce made a habit of going there a lot. She'd help the librarians out with tasks, and they all fell in love with her. So much so that when the library held one of their coffee-and-cookies programs for the trustees, the head librarian asked little Joyce if she'd like to give a presentation on a book she'd read.

Well, Joyce and I prepared for that for so long, we must have looked insane. But I worked with her until Joyce had

*My daughter Joyce
getting a bath in the
sink. How cute!*

her essay down perfect. We got her a darling new dress and shoes, and we fixed her hair so she'd look completely adorable. I couldn't wait to bask in my daughter's triumph.

You can probably see where this is going.

Joyce got up in front of the ladies, looking as cute as can be, and when they said, "Okay, Joyce, you can start," she started shifting. Then she starts getting busy with her hands. She's looking around.

"Joyce, get going," I'm thinking.

She starts talking, and out comes nothing that resembles what we'd worked on. She's ad-libbing like crazy, looking at everybody and smiling like she knows what she's saying, but it was obvious to everybody what had happened. The group was really sweet about it, but I kept thinking, "I'm gonna kill her when I get home!"

Maybe this story is more about me and my reaction than my daughter. Sorry, Joyce!

The thing to remember, though, is that while I probably got a little too mad that day, I can laugh about it now. Everybody gets stage fright, and she'd never spoken in front of people before. Besides, I couldn't have been prouder of the fact that Joyce learned how to get over her stage fright, because she went on to become a wonderful teacher. I mean, you *have* to be able to take charge of a room in that job!

I AM MAGGIE,
HEAR ME ROAR

Boy, is it time for a woman to be president. [*Amen, sister! Preach! Oh shit, I hope she's not talking about Sarah Palin.*]

Guys are so nuts (all this fooling around they do when they're in office) that it's time to give a woman a chance. I just don't think a girl would be so crazy if she were in that job. If Hillary Clinton had gotten on the ticket in 2008, I would have voted for her. [*Whew.*] She's tough, and she's obviously very, very smart, and I think you need somebody who's both to be president. I love her. [*Just to clarify, my mom did vote for Obama, and yes I got her a little tipsy before driving her to the polling place.*]

Kathy likes to call me an "early feminist" because of my belief in the power of women. Also, I guess, because I had the kind of marriage in which we shared duties across the board. Johnny helped change diapers; I handled the money.

[*That sounds like a disparity in the distribution of power, Mom, but good for you.*] And when I took a job because we needed extra money, Johnny helped pick up the slack when it came to household chores like getting dinners ready and putting kids to bed. I spoke up when I needed help, and because I married a great guy, I got it. But on top of that, my daughters never heard from me that a woman couldn't do anything she set her mind to. I'm all for women climbing that ladder as far as they want to go. I mean, my editor on this book is a woman! And her boss is a woman! That's great. Kathy's a boss, too, to that lovely Tom and Tiffany. Hopefully Tiffany will be a boss someday! [*Hopefully Tiffany will be changing my diapers someday. And Mom calling Tom "lovely" just never gets old.*]

You could say we've come a long way since the days when my dad could forbid his girls from being "unladylike" in his house. [*Her dad had sixteen children. As if that wonderful old mick could even keep track.*] Once, when I was living in that apartment with Irene (we were both married with kids and our husbands were in the service then), I had to run over to my dad's store—not very far away—to get something for the baby. It was a hot summer day, and I had a little shirt and shorts on, and I scuttled through the alley so nobody would see me.

I go in, and my dad says, "What are you doing walking around like that?"

Immediately I became a kid again. "Dad!"

We needed stuff for the kids, but I tried to make it sound as tragic and dire as possible to excuse myself. "I had to get milk, Dad!" Here I was, a grown woman, married, a mother, and I felt ten years old all over again.

"You're not leaving this store and this house with those on," he said, referring to my shorts, which probably went past my knees, considering the era.

"Oh, all right," I said. Dad would naturally throw in a few extra items for us whenever I bought something from his store because he was a very kind man, but he had old-fashioned ideas about women, so I still had to trudge back wearing one of my mother's aprons, because what I had on wasn't what a mother wore even to run a quick errand. God forbid! I was able to laugh about it as I made my way back to Irene—back through the alley, of course—looking more appropriate in my father's eyes for a married woman. [*Next up for the coalition forces (after they rout those sexist Taliban): 1930s Chicago.*]

"Oh good," Irene said when I got back and told her what happened. "I'm so glad you went instead of me!" [*Irene, snap!*]

Now, do I think girls who get married should go out to a dance club with their girlfriends? No. Movies, dinner together, sure. But what are you going dancing for if you're married? Guys are going to ask you to dance, and what are you going to do then? [*Throw your drink in their face, that's what. The nerve. And in a dance club!*] You've got a husband at home. Be smart. [Real Housewives of Orange County, *meet Maggie, the hottest housewife ever!*]

Also, I'm not so nutsy a feminist that a guy complimenting me at work on how I look puts me in a lather. [*Not a leather?*] When you're young and pretty, a guy might say, "Hey, babe, you know you look pretty sexy in that dress!" I don't think that's so bad. [*Unless you'd prefer to abide by Title VII of the 1964 Civil Rights Act.*] When it's done respectfully. I was the hot new babe at Form Fit Bra Factory when I started working there after high school, and I tell ya, that attention felt pretty good. Now you hear, "Oh! I want to sue for a million dollars!" Geez. [*Uh-oh. I hope Levi Johnston can't read this.*]

But don't get me wrong. A guy who wants to get all scrungy about it, and pinch you maybe, or get really graphic, then you go up and slap him. [*Unless you'd prefer to abide by the country's assault and battery laws.*] Don't take any of that nonsense. I don't go for that crap. One time I didn't even have to slap the guy. I was working in a doctor's office, and there was an optometrist whose big thing was to head straight to my desk and tell me dirty jokes. I was married and with a couple kids. I don't know what that louse thought he was getting away with.

Well, I never laughed. Underneath, I'd do all my hating. "Hey scumbag," I'd say in my mind. But outwardly, I'd say "Oh gosh!" and then turn back to what I was doing. Or not say anything and just keep working. Then one day this optometrist came over, started one of his kneeslappers, and stopped himself. [*This guy sounds like such an asshole.*]

"You know, I think I'm wasting my time here," he said. "Margaret never seems to appreciate my jokes." [*Never mind. I'm totally on his side now.*]

"Doctor, I have a lot of work to do, and I just don't have time for it," I said.

He never came up to me again. I showed my displeasure without yelling or screaming. I just gave him the cold shoulder, and wouldn't give him the satisfaction of the tiniest laugh. That did it. [*Maybe I'm missing the lesson here, but she could have at least gotten a free eye exam.*]

Look, I'm very much a feminist when it comes to women not taking any abuse from men. Ever. I always say, a husband might hit me once. But twice, never, because either I'd kill him or he'd be in jail for the rest of his life. I want all women to respect themselves, get as good an education as they can, and not stand for any mistreatment from friends, bosses, and men in general. Don't settle, ladies!

That means I've also long believed in equal pay for men and women. [*Whoa, is that the sound of your boyfriend Bill O'Reilly breaking up with you?*] My view on that came about when I worked part-time at the hospital. We had a fella who quit his job, and to replace him they picked this girl who had worked with him, because she was really excellent. She was next in line for it, and it was smart of the hospital to give the job to her. Then I found out she was being paid almost $4,000 less than he was making. How could you not think that wasn't fair?

But in my day, the man was the breadwinner, and when women worked, it was for "fun." [*Or to be sexually harassed a teeny bit.*] Or it was for a specific need. I mean, I went to work because Johnny and I realized tuition fees for the kids' high school were looming [*here we go*], and we wanted our kids to go to Catholic high school. [*Yeah, that one really "took."*] I knew one woman who worked to pay for a daughter's wedding. And I remember another woman telling me she was working because her family needed a new refrigerator. But four years later, she was still working. You have to think, maybe after that refrigerator was paid for, she liked the satisfaction of having a good job and doing it well, even if it meant rearranging her home life. [*Or she wanted to buy refrigerators for the whole block.*]

I asked my colleague who wasn't making as much as her male predecessor why she didn't say something about the pay fairness. "Oh, I don't want to say anything," she said. "I'm delighted I have this good job." [*As I expect my staff—or as I call them, laborers—to say.*]

But nowadays, women are often the breadwinners, because they're maybe divorced with a kid and got screwed by a guy who isn't paying his share. Single moms have to work, and they're fighting for equal pay.

I will say that I don't think a woman should have to be too strong or too tough to succeed. I don't like the idea that women have to act like men to get their way. [*Fine. I'll tuck my penis under for this part of the chapter.*] I think you can be a woman and be strong and be respected but still be compassionate and feeling, and not have to prove yourself as being tough like a man. If you're smart, your smarts will usually come out on their own. Look at Eleanor Roosevelt, a first lady I just loved. She used to write a column for newspapers and magazines; I was in my teens when it started running, and I always read it. She was so smart, and wrote about important topics of the day, things affecting everyday people and families, but also subjects empowering to women, like discrimination and the Equal Rights Amendment, which I'm in favor of. Eleanor was a woman who wasn't about spending money on clothes, or simply looking proper as the wife of the president. A lot of times, who I like in a president has a lot to do with who they're married to. [*That's why Sarah Palin has such a following. It's a-a-a-ll about Todd.*]

I wasn't so crazy about the man-hating that went on when the women's movement got big, though. Maybe that's because I married a great guy. Irene and Rae did, too. My brothers were great guys. Sure, there were scuzzy guys around the neighborhood, but you just didn't pay attention to them.

And don't get me started on the bra burners. What was that supposed to mean? We all need a bra at some point. It was probably the eighteen-year-olds who were doing that, because they didn't need them. The rest of us? We needed them. And that bra-burning idea was right up the guys' alley, wasn't it? Guys loved that.

Push Up Your Fofties

KATHY: Wait a second, Mom. I just want to get out there that the bra-burning thing was kind of a myth.

MAGGIE: Good. Because it sounded stupid.

K: But can we divulge one of the real reasons you loved a good bra?

M: What do you mean?

K: Your getting-out-of-a-ticket method?

M: Oh. Right.

K: What would you tell me about how to make that nice police officer dismiss my speeding ticket?

M: Well, you say, in a real sweet voice, "Oh Officer, I'm really sorry." You never argue with a cop. Never.

K: It's kind of like being raped. Just do what they say and wait till it's over.

M: No, no! Kathleen! You act all innocent, say you're sorry, and then, you know, you give them a reason to maybe forget about the ticket.

K: And that reason is . . . I wish I had a drum roll.

M: You push up your fofties.

K: "Fofties"! Boobs, Mom. I don't know where you got "fofties."

M: You just kind of lean back a little, push 'em up, bat your eyelashes, and say, "Oh Officer, I'm just so sorry. I was very upset."

K: "My giant boobs fell on the steering wheel and caused me to make that wrong turn."

M: That's right.

K: Did this ever actually work?

M: Well, a few times Dad and I were driving somewhere . . .

K: Whoa, whoa, whoa. How does that method work when Dad's in the car?

M: Well, in that case, he sees two older people . . .

K: Pushing up their fofties. Dad had fofties by then. Quite a pair, too.

M: My fofties had kind of gone by that point.

K: Also, how does this work if it's a lady officer? They have them, you know.

M: "You've got beautiful eyelashes" maybe?

K: Yeah, that's gonna knock down the price of that ticket real fast.

M: Look, you're never getting that ticket torn up if it's a woman cop.

K: Not even if it's a lesbian?

M: I doubt it. Don't you think they'd be into following the law?

Look, men can sometimes be so nuts about sex. A guy'll have a wonderful wife, everything you'd ever want, money to burn, be at the top of his profession, and then go and do something stupid. It happens so often with men, you have to wonder what it's all about. I just don't think women would pull that kind of goofy stuff so often. Of course, every time I read about a woman screwing up, I can't help but think, "She's screwing it up for all women!" Because certainly with men, when they make mistakes—especially of the fooling around on the side kind—you sense there's a lot of nudging elbows and smiles among other men. It's why I've been known to say, "Men are such pigs!" and then get razzed about saying that by my own kids. "Ma says men are all pigs!" I don't really think that. [*Wait, what?*]

But if you're a young girl and you get PG [*that's pregnant, youngsters, not the movie rating*], you know that guy will be out of sight so fast, you're going to be the one suffering. And that's the truth. [*Clearly Mom hasn't missed one episode of MTV's monster hit* 16 and Pregnant.]

If You Never Have Sex, You Never Get Pregnant

KATHY: Okay, Mom, hold on. I think everyone should know about your birds and bees talk with me.

MAGGIE: Oh dear, that must have been choice.

K: Do you remember? I had a worksheet and the assignment was, I was supposed to have a discussion with my parents.

M: Oh God . . .

K: You were supposed to talk to me about the birds and the bees, and there was stuff you were supposed to fill in on the worksheet. She was a progressive teacher, which I thought was great. My one hippie teacher.

M: Which I probably didn't think was so great.

K: Come on, Mom. What happened? You were on the phone with Irene . . .

M: Uh-oh.

K: Yeah, that's right, "Uh-oh." When you're on the phone with Irene, all bets are off. Everyone has to be quiet. We didn't have "time out" in those days. But were you careful not to use negative words with children? What did you do?

TIP
IT!

M: I probably put my hand over the phone . . .

K: That's right . . .

M: . . . and said, "Shut your mouth." Or whatever. Something very genteel like that. You're right, we didn't have time out.

K: Or supernannies to put us in a no-no area. When you were mad at the kids, what did you say? "Wait till your father gets home," right?

M: Poor John. It didn't happen that often. But sometimes he'd come home from work, and I'd open the door and say, "John, you've got to do something with" whoever. Then Dad would say, "What happened?" And I'd say, "Well, one of them did this." Then he'd go and talk to the kids, and of course it's always different when the father talks to the kids. 'Cause Mom, she's yappin' all day long, saying "Don't do this" and "Don't do that." When the father talks to the kids, though, you get results right away.

K: By the way, that's why you're not a feminist leader.

M: I never knew how to get results.

K: No, Mom. It's because you shouldn't say that a woman "yaps" all day, but when a *father* "talks," it means something.

M: But it's the truth.

K: Okay, Maggie Steinem. And what's with telling everyone it's okay if a guy says "You look sexy today" to a girl at work?

M: I don't think that's terrible. These girls get so offended, my gosh . . .

K: How would you feel if Tom said to Tiffany, "Hey Toots, hot outfit" every day?

M: Well, you're not supposed to make a practice of it. You say it once in a while.

K: As Tiffany's boss, I guess it's appropriate, then, for me to say, "For sexual favors, Tiff, you'll get a raise." But only once in a while. Every first Wednesday of the month, maybe? That's your line of thinking.

M: Oh sure, that's fine. That's exactly what I meant, Kathy.

K: Look, I'm getting sidetracked. Our birds and the bees talk. Do you remember it being, say, a lengthy conversation?

M: No, I will say that. It's probably why I don't remember much of it.

K: You had your hand over the phone because you were talking to Irene.

M: I was probably sitting on the little stool.

K: Wearing?

M: A duster.

K: Yes! So I've asked you for a birds and bees talk, I'm handing you a worksheet, you're on the phone, you put your hand over it, and said?

M: Something wise, surely.

K: You barked, "The word is 'no.' If you don't ever have sex, you won't ever get pregnant." End of discussion. And then back to Irene.

M: Well, we had important things to talk about.

K: I was in high school, Mom. I needed that talk. For several years afterward I was a little confused about what goes where and why. How you explained anatomy to me was, if you never have sex, you never get pregnant. "Just say no" long before Nancy Reagan.

M: There you go, I might not have been a feminist pioneer, but I was a sex education one.

K: Well, because of that I had to learn about my period from the streets, Mom. The cold hard streets of Oak Park, Illinois. I hope you and Irene solved a lot of problems that day.

M: Well, we probably did.

I know Kathy likes to provoke me, but the reality is, what she does as a comedian is pretty brave, and I look up to her. As a woman—a very smart woman—she's a role model, I think. That doesn't mean I'm okay with the more controversial things she says, because I think sometimes it hurts her. But she's braver than I could ever be in a million years. And a lot braver than other comics, who are afraid to say the stuff she says. Even when a lot of them are thinking it themselves! [*Written just the way I wanted you to put it, Mom!*]

There are a lot of pretentious people out there who think they're soooo high and mighty, and they need a little bit of what Kathy gives them. [*And in Oprah's case, a lot.*]

Also, for all the guff she gets about how foul-mouthed she is, she isn't half as disgusting as a lot of these male comics. I do think she gets a bit of a bad rap, because sometimes they'll fish out this stuff she says or does and harp about it in the papers and on television, when guy comics are ten times as filthy. And usually at the expense of women. The way women are degraded by male comics is just disgusting. [*I'm looking at you, Jerry Seinfeld, you disgusting filthmonger. Just stop with the pussy jokes already!*]

Which brings me back to Hillary [*what?*], and how female politicians are dealt with. I think she was treated abominably on the campaign trail most of the time. Just awful. Here's a smart, tough woman with as good credentials as anybody for the Oval Office, and she was ridiculed for stuff you'd never see a guy get made fun of for, like fashion and looks. When did we start this ridiculing of people? Can't we go back to being civilized about all this?

Take what happened to that Sarah Palin when she was picked to be John McCain's running mate in the 2008 election. I really got mad—and still get mad—at the way people treat her. [*Oh no. No, no, no. Levi, hold me!*] It was unfair to throw her out there unprepared, just because they wanted

TIP
IT!

a woman out there. Then they go and pick somebody unqualified. She's been catapulted into a situation where she's just made so much fun of, and now nobody wants her around. Certainly not for president, which is what I understand she's maybe looking toward.

Well, she can want what she wants, but she has to prove she can do it. [*Not until someone proves to her there's a difference between North and South Korea.*]

She really should take a lesser job, like mayor of Wasilla. She's already done it. She was fine at it. What was wrong with that? That still seems like a good job to me. She certainly knows more than I do about being a mayor. [*But you know more than she does about wine, so you're even.*]

MAGGIE'S BEAUTY TIPS

My beauty philosophy is simple. It's MLV, which stands for the only three things a nice girl [*or gay*] needs in her purse for all her beauty needs:

MASCARA—to bring out your eyes. Don't use too much, you don't want to appear loose.

LIPSTICK—to make your lips look dignified (go easy on the lipstick, too, as too much will turn you into a tramp); lipstick is also perfect to use on your cheeks as rouge.

VASELINE—an excellent moisturizer. Also great to keep your lips and hands soft.

Note: EYEBROW PENCIL *may* be added to the MLV beauty kit, but only for extremely fancy occasions.

USE IT UP, WEAR IT OUT,
MAKE IT DO

"*M*a, the Depression's over!"

That's what I hear from my kids when I try to tell them about the era in which I grew up. Like a tattoo on your brain, the Great Depression, which hit us all in 1929 and lasted into the 1940s, was the kind of experience that can give you a lot of know-how in being wise about money.

"You paid WHAT for that?" I'll say when they tell me about something they bought.

Here it comes: "Ma, the Depression's over."

Well, guess what? The Depression kinda came right back these last two years, didn't it?

I'm in my glory! Now I can say, "I told you so!"

Let me tell you about the kind of thing I saw when I was a kid during those horrible, horrible times. I remember women coming into my dad's store, crying and begging my dad for groceries for their families. Really crying, I tell ya. Now, these were people who might not have been able to pay my father for three weeks running, but being the very kind man he was, he always helped out. "My husband is out of a job" is what he'd hear from these weeping women. "And we have a couple of kids."

But sometimes my dad would feel like reminding them, "I still have kids to raise myself."

Seeing that made an impression on me. I told myself, "I hope I never have to beg anybody to give me groceries to feed my kids."

We had a big family. We weren't rich by any means. But my dad was a serious businessman. Every night, when he would lay out all the cash from the day in neat piles of bills before taking it to the bank, you couldn't bother him. This was serious stuff. No asking how much was there, no talking to him at all. But I'd watch him, fascinated.

He knew how to economize, I tell ya. We weren't allowed to touch the thermostat. Oh, no. And if you tried to open a window when it was cold, he would come in, shut that window, and say, "I'm not paying to heat the outside."

That makes it sound like he was a stickler, but I have to say, the way he handled money allowed him to help all of us go to school, buy homes, get started in businesses, marriages, and all that. We had nice Christmases—nothing extravagant, but we got good gifts—and we always got new clothes for Easter. And my parents were taking care of quite a few kids, may I remind you, never less than five in the household at any one time. But we never felt like we wanted for anything.

We got allowances all the time, too. When I was in grammar school, I would get a quarter each Saturday and Sunday. And boy, what I could do with that quarter! The movies were a dime, and everything you'd want in the way of candy or snacks was a nickel. With the extra dime, though, I'd see if I could take a girlfriend of mine who maybe didn't have the money to pay for a movie. And if I was alone, believe me, I could sure fill myself up on junk for fifteen cents.

But a quarter today? Can it get you anything?

Everything is so expensive now that when Kathy used to tell me about something she bought and what it cost, I'd say, "Don't, Kathy. Stop. I can't listen. I feel faint." She knows not to even bring up what she pays for things anymore. Sometimes I accidentally find out, and it makes me nuts. She bought me new towels recently—you know, the set that includes a big bath towel, a medium-size towel, and a little hand-size one—and I noticed that the price tag was still on the hand towel. Eighteen bucks! For the smallest towel! I didn't say anything to her, but all I could think of was what that $18 would have gotten me when I was raising my kids. Two sets of towels easily!

And bread, good God. I picked up a loaf of bread by mistake at the grocery store recently, and when I got to the counter, I found out that it was $3.89! Now, I went ahead and bought it. But not without a whole lot of "What am I doing?" going around in my head. Even I go a little crazy sometimes, readers.

At least I'm not spending those godawful prices for coffee they charge at these hip coffee places. When I think of so many working young people spending their money on coffee, it's ridiculous. It doesn't leave them any money for more important things. Like paying their bills?

When I got older, and started to work, my mother laid down the basics.

"Pay your expenses. Always save something. The rest you spend."

And that's what I always did.

I graduated from high school in 1938, and when I started getting a steady paycheck at the Form Fit Bra Factory as a secretary in the returns department, my mother made me open a little savings account. She'd say, "Go cash your check, put it in the bank right away, and you're done." Then I made sure I paid my mother room and board.

Yes, that's right. I paid my mother room and board for living at home. Everybody who lived at home did that in my day. I made $12 a week, and I paid my mother $3. I still had money for nice clothes, for going out on weekends, and that fifteen-cent cola at work for lunch. (But I brought my lunch, so I saved there, too!)

TIP
IT!

See, parents in our day didn't want their children to be raised as freeloaders. They figured, if you were old enough to get a job, you were old enough to pay for where you slept and ate, even if that was at home. In my family, there was a secret catch, though, which made a big difference. When any of us left to get an apartment, Dad would give back that money to put toward the apartment. He didn't really need it, you see. What he and Mom wanted to do was teach us a lesson in responsibility. It was a savings account all this time, only you didn't know it.

Dad was great when it came to helping any of us out. But then, families had to work together. There was no unemployment insurance, no welfare. Everybody was dependent on one another. It was wonderful, really, the way family members took care of one another. If one of my older brothers was having a tough time—with the heating bill, maybe, or food—the rest of the family would help him. Or you'd see kids taking care of a widowed mom if the husband died. As my mother said, you never want to see your kids—or anybody in your family—go without. Especially if there are grandkids involved. It was a spirit about helping out that made us all pitch in. None of us had that much as it was. But that's just what you did.

Nobody ever looked at their parents as a bank, either. That's because you never had to ask them for money most of the time. Mom or Dad would come to you, instead. "How are you doing?" one of them would say on a regular basis. If you and your spouse were looking to buy a house, then they'd help. That's what they felt their money was for, as long as you were doing your part about not being foolish with money. My parents worked too hard for their money to throw it away. But if it was for something good and substantial, they were just wonderful. My dad helped I don't know how many of us buy homes, or get into small businesses.

That was how I wanted to be. Thrifty, but with a purpose. We never wanted for anything during a hard time, and I hoped to do the same thing when I had my own family.

When Johnny and I were young marrieds, we lived from paycheck to paycheck. But as our family grew, and Johnny started making more money, we ended up doing pretty well. That's because we paid our bills, watched our finances, and learned to save.

This may sound strange, but I love paying bills. My kids always say, "You're the only one I know who's ever happy about paying bills." You know why? Because I actually like having electricity. I want light, and gas, and a roof over my head! Legitimate bills? You won't see me complaining when I'm writing those checks. Those begging moms in my dad's store were all the motivation I needed.

Of course, in my younger days people paid their bills in cash and in person. The hardware store up the street would take your gas and electric bills, I remember. Then Johnny and

I got a checking account, and we paid by mail. I was the one who took care of our household expenses, as most women did in my day. The guys made the money, but they didn't necessarily want to get involved in spending it. Of course, I loved that, because it let me be like my dad when he was working with those piles of money. It wasn't cash I was staring at on the table—it was bills—but I had the money to pay them, and that was the best part!

It's important for married people to communicate with each other about expenses. How else are you going to be on the same page about money? Johnny never questioned anything about bill-paying, but I always let him know the status of our accounts. Sometimes, the expenses were high enough that we'd have to cut down on going out, or seeing shows, and Johnny was always agreeable.

Then there'd be those times when you looked at your budget and realized, we can go out this weekend! We can have company over! We're doing real well! Whichever the case, we were always happy. Because we were in it together.

Credit cards—they're terrible, and they're wonderful. They've ruined everything, and yet when you have one with you, you feel safe. That's the paradox.

Having a credit card with me means I know I've got money for whatever comes up. Emergency-wise, that is. When you're stuck in the middle of nowhere, for instance, and you need a place to stay for the night. Or you suddenly get stuck with a costly emergency.

But it's disgusting the way they're hurting everybody now. It's half the problem with the country today. When I hear about some credit debt people have, I can't believe it! How can you sleep when you owe twenty, thirty, forty, or fifty thousand dollars? It would drive me nuts. I feel sorry for people in this predicament, because they've obviously never learned how to use a credit card.

People of my generation didn't grow up with credit cards, incidentally. We had something called layaway, though. When you put something on layaway, you didn't get it till you'd made your last payment. No taking it home first. Let's say you wanted a nice dress for a party coming up. You made sure you paid it off before that party, or you wouldn't have that dress in time.

But when credit cards first came out, I remember how wonderful it was to have one. We had a Sears card, and it meant you didn't always have to have cash for everything when you shopped there. My daughter Joyce was a kid then, and when I would take her to buy her Easter clothes, or new clothes for school, I'd hand the credit card to the cashier, and Joyce would say, "Oh, Mommy, this is so nice! You don't have to pay for anything!"

I'd have to say to her, "Well yes, Joyce, I do. I have to pay later."

It was too complicated to explain to a little girl. But adults? They should know better. Too many are just paying the minimum and that's it! It's appalling. See, back in my day, the credit card you got was for a very small amount of credit, maybe only a few hundred dollars. And when you reached that limit, you couldn't get any more credit until the bill was fully paid. Sounds like a good idea, huh? I swear, sometimes it just seems like all the good ideas went away.

It's become too easy for people to get credit cards, and everybody knows that now. Loans became too easy to get, too. In my day, if you wanted to buy a house, say, you'd save and save and save and then go to a bank, hoping you had enough for a down payment. Then maybe the bank would say, "No, you don't have quite enough yet. You need a little more. Then come back and talk to us." How things have changed. When I heard about people putting no money down to get a house, I thought, how does that even make sense? It's the same with credit cards. Why let just anybody have one?

Johnny and I always knew the value of a credit card. Even as our line of credit increased, we made sure to use it only for a big item, something we needed that we didn't have all the cash for at that time, or for a trip. Look, I'd never have gotten to go to Europe if I didn't have a credit card. On any trip, a credit card really came in handy. But when that bill came, I would make sure I paid that off in three or four installments at the most. That was it. The faster, the better. I didn't want to see that unpaid debt any longer than I had to.

Believe me, here's the deal with credit cards. You better pay sooner, or you will *really* pay later.

"Use it up, wear it out, make it do."

That's another one of my thrifty tips. My kids might roll their eyes at how often they've heard it, but I didn't make it up. That was a popular saying during the Depression. "Use it up, wear it out, make it do, or do without." Everyone learned the importance of being frugal then: patching up clothes before you bought new ones, keeping things until they just gave out, and wasting nothing. Winston Churchill even said it to the people of England during World War II when times were tough. Why do you need that new thing when the one you have works fine? I feel that way every time one of my kids tells me about some new piece of electronics they bought. Or you see these people trade out a perfectly good refridge for one of those stainless steel kind that makes ice and looks fancy. Or switching out the TV for one of those flat kinds, and then that flat kind for a bigger flat kind. Don't they all show you the same thing anyway?

We never did that, and I don't see why people do it now.

Well, okay, I sort of do. One problem now is that things aren't made to stand the test of time. Products used to last a lifetime. You'd be happy if you lived as long as your stove did. Now everything is junk. Recently, I was talking to a woman my age—like me, the Depression is a favorite topic for her—and she was telling me about how her daughter's been through three toasters in just a few years, but the one *she* grew up with lasted almost twenty!

Not that Johnny and I ever made our kids afraid to spend money. But we wanted them to know that if money was being spent on something, they should use that thing. Or at least take care of it.

I still bring this one up to Kathy. When she was in grammar school, I bought her what the kids used to call a poncho. [*They're still called that, Mom.*] You know, that article of clothing with a hole in the middle that your head goes in? They're warm, and you can take them off easy, and they're real cute. Well, they were all the rage, and I bought her one. Paid maybe $18 for it. God, what was I thinking? Anyway, she was really proud of it, and she wore it to school. Then the weather turned a little, and she took it off and threw it on the fence. The bell rang for school to start and she ran in, and later remembered she'd left the poncho outside. Well, the sister wouldn't let her go out to see if it was still there, so she came home after school and said, "I can't find the poncho."

We trudged back to the school, looking everywhere for it, her crying and me half yelling at her about why she couldn't leave it where she could see it! Naturally some kid found it, thought, "What a nice poncho!" and took it home. I'm sure

Kathy still thinks about that poncho. I certainly do my part to help her think about it.

"Remember the poncho you got to wear only once?" I'll say.

Use it up, wear it out, make it do, everyone. Or do without!

An Old-Fashioned Flimflam Scam

KATHY: I know another one of your budget tips, Mom.

MAGGIE: What?

K: Perhaps you'd like to tell everyone about how good you are at returning things.

M: Well, working in the returns department at Form Fit was very valuable experience. See, I would write letters to people who sent us the bras they'd purchased, and—

K: Hold on, hold on, Mom. I'm talking about what you do now. Let me throw out a hypothetical. Let's say you had a daughter whom we'll just call—oh, I don't know—Bathy. And every single year for Christmas, Bathy got you a new sweater or a new outfit or a new makeup kit that she thought you would like, and then every single year without fail, that new sweater or outfit or makeup kit somehow ended up back at the store. Would you like to walk us through that process?

M: The reason is, Kathy, the things you gave me—

K: *B*athy, Mom.

M: Oh, stop it. Look, those gifts were too expensive! I didn't want you to spend that kind of money.

K: What. Do. You. Care. I got it for you!

M: I do care, Kathy, because I want you to save your money.

K: But you pocket the money anyway!

M: But I know what I want. I could probably buy three things for the one thing you paid for.

K: It's a scam, Mom. An old-fashioned flimflam scam.

M: What do I need with these fancy things you buy for me? You bought me a Coach bag, and a beautiful blazer, with some slacks to go with it, and you said, "This will be wonderful when you go shopping." Shopping? I look like a slob when I go shopping, and that's the way I like it.

K: How do you talk the salesgirl into giving you cash when you know I paid credit for it?

M: I don't know. I just do.

K: Fess up.

M: I just tell them I want cash.

K: And? You what? Come on. You told me this. You act piti-
ful and . . .

M: Bat my eyelashes.

K: There. Was that so hard?

M: Well, you've *got* to bat the eyelashes.

But I'll tell you one of the reasons I'm very proud of Kathy.
When we moved out to Los Angeles from Chicago, Kathy
came, too, and stayed with us until she was twenty-eight.
That's because she wanted to break into showbiz, and we didn't
want her worrying about money. But when she got her first
apartment—a little studio place—she was thrilled to pieces,
and we were thrilled, too.

So I did what my mother did for me: showed her how to
make a budget for herself. See, when Kathy made money
while she was living with us, she only had to worry about
spending for herself. We never charged her room and board,
and we let her use our car and our gas card. We paid her
medical bills, and I even tucked a five-dollar bill in the rear-
view mirror for her, so when she went out with her friends
after acting class she had some money for fries and a Coke,
perhaps. I never wanted her to be without money.

But when she moved out, I wanted to pass on what I'd
learned; she was going to be living on her own and paying

for things on her own. I had done the same thing for all my kids when they left home. I showed her how to keep different envelopes for different expenses; how to prioritize from what gets paid first (rent, utilities, credit card debt) to what gets paid last (clothing, eating out); how it's important to save even just a little from your paycheck, because it could ultimately help you pay for something bigger; how you shouldn't rob Peter to pay Paul. All my wisdom from being a budget-conscious Depression-era child. Then we sent her off to live on her own.

I sat down next to my husband afterward and said, "I know what's going to happen. I can tell you, every other month, she'll be comin' with 'I don't have the rent! I can't pay the electric bill!' "

"It's still a good idea, what you did, Mag," Johnny said to me. "That's your thing. That's what you love to do."

So I waited for that call. And waited. And waited.

I never got it.

She never once came to us for rent money, for utilities, for anything like that. Remember, this was a kid, money didn't mean anything to her. Believe me. And Kathy just did wonderful. I was so proud of her.

Of course, now I think she spends way too much money on things.

But she's got it at least!

MAGGIE'S THRIFTY TIPS FOR GOING GREEN

In my day, we didn't say "recycling," we called it "conserving." Here are some surefire ways to conserve the planet!

1. REUSE PAPER TOWELS. No need to buy those silly half-size paper towels, just buy full-size, rinse them out, and wring them dry after you use them. Hang them over the side of the counter to dry and they will be good as new in a day. If it's just wrinkled, so what? Are you too fancy for wrinkled?

2. SAVE RUBBER BANDS. Didn't you know there's a rubber shortage going on? Every ten thousand of those useful little elastic helpers you don't throw away will save a tire!

3. REUSE GREETING CARDS. Just because a card has been signed once doesn't mean you can't use your God-given creative talents to make it new! Draw over that old signature and turn it into a bunch of flowers or a pretty paisley-patterned heart and sign that card again. Your original artwork will make the recipient feel extra-special.

4. USE A TISSUE TILL IT FALLS APART. If you're real careful with how you fold a tissue you can use it to blow your nose up to ten times!

TIP
IT!

5.	WEAR A MUUMUU OR A DUSTER. When you're at home a duster is the ultimate in comfort, and for a garden party you only have to get half-assed dressed up, so a muumuu is the perfect outfit. You can wear 'em a hundred times between washings, which is only three and a half washes a year. Think of all that water and laundry soap you'll save!

6.	DRINK BOX WINE. According to fancy environmental experts, a three-liter box of wine generates half the emissions that manufacturing and shipping a 750-milliliter bottle of wine produces. Plus, you get more wine!

MY BOYS BILL AND ANDERSON

Maybe you remember when my daughter said that terrible, terrible thing at the Emmys a few years ago about Jesus. I guess, it was more *to* Jesus—well, both about and to Jesus, really—but anyway, I won't be reprinting it here. [*"Suck it, Jesus" is what I said. I repeat it often.*] Let's just say I wasn't too happy. I was happy for her winning the award, of course, but not about how she handled herself. This was television, for Chrissakes! People are watching! [*By people, she means the tens of viewers who watch a clip special that airs on the E! channel on Saturday morning a week before the prime-time Emmy Awards.*]

Well, pretty soon after that I was watching my beloved Bill O'Reilly [*Zzzzzz, huh, what?*] on his Fox show *The O'Reilly Factor,* and when he got to his "Pinheads and Patriots" segment, he mentioned Kathy, then showed the clip of what she said when she was onstage accepting her Emmy. He even warned his viewers to change the channel, because they might find it offensive! [*I support all changing of channels from Fox News to anything else.*] Well, I already knew what she was going to say, so I kept it right there.

After the clip, he said the words I knew were coming: "Ms. Griffin is a pinhead, no doubt."

Guess what, Bill? I couldn't have agreed with you more! [*Is that a bus I hear? Because I believe I was just thrown under it by my own mother.*]

I even thought it was funny when he showed a clip of Joy Behar and Kathy talking about something political, and he called them Dumb and Dumber. I thought that was hysterical! Not that I'd ever call Kathy dumb. Reckless, maybe. Never dumb.

Maybe that's why I love my Bill O'Reilly. He tells it like he sees it, which is what I do, and what I did, too, to Kathy after she blurted out that awful thing at the Emmys, and used that bad language on New Year's Eve with Anderson Cooper, and . . . oh there're too many examples to go into. I know Kathy and my other kids—mostly liberals, all—get on my case about watching Bill. But I don't care. He's got an excellent speaking voice, always looks real handsome, and is on the lookout for these idiots who want to hurt us. He's got a lot of things to say about morals and the way our country should be that I have to admit I agree with. (I like Sean Hannity, too. He seems like he'd be the perfect son. Of course, they're both Irish Catholic, so maybe I'm a little prejudiced!)

[Mom, can you choose a word other than "prejudiced"? How about "fluffy"?]

Now, do I sometimes hear something Bill says and roll my eyes and say, "Oh, Bill, come on!"? Sure! And he does talk over his guests a little too much to suit me. And I guess there was that one little episode on his old tabloidy show *Inside Edition* that made its way around the Internet recently (and which Kathy was only too happy to show me), where he's screaming at somebody—using bad language that I know he doesn't really approve of—and he clearly thinks it'll never be recorded for posterity. He must have been under a lot of stress or something. *[The stress of counting his money and sending angry e-mails to that terrorist George Clooney.]* But who agrees with everything somebody they like says or does? Plus, some of these people are so far out with their opinions, to me they're actually funny. I can't even get mad at what they're saying because it's so stupid.

Ever since I started watching *The O'Reilly Factor*—I never saw Bill on *Inside Edition*—I've found him to be very smart and very funny. I also think he's fair and balanced. *[It's not like you made that phrase up, Mom. You're spouting a Fox News slogan.]* To a point. He says he's not a Republican, that he's an Independent. But he does lean toward the conservative side. And there's nothing wrong with that. I've leaned that way myself as I've gotten older. But at heart, I consider myself Independent, too. *[For the record, my mother's a registered member of the Bullshit Party.]*

If you listened to my kids, though, they'd lead you to think I listened to his radio show every day, too, I was some rah-rah Republican, and had posters of Bill on the wall!

Okay, everyone, I do have a doormat that says THE SPIN STOPS HERE that Kathleen ordered for me from an Internet catalogue. [*Yeah, Mom, I paid for it with S&H green stamps.*] And I have a signed picture of him, too. Those of you who watch Kathy's show know that. One day I went over to Kathy's house and she said, "I've got a surprise for you!" I've learned over the years to not know what that might possibly mean. Since the cameras were there to film, I just assumed she was going to say something to get me riled up. But instead she hands me this big envelope, and inside is this glossy picture of my Bill—a real nice shot, I tell ya—and a nice message made out to me!

Well, I let out a scream, like I was a teenage girl! And I never do that.

I still haven't gotten it framed yet—sorry, Bill! [*Yeah, Bill, hope we haven't inconvenienced you, BILL.*] But every once in a while I take it out and look at it and laugh. Not at you, Bill! [*Oh no, Bill. No one in this house would ever laugh AT you. We laugh WITH you. Especially your hilariously witty repartee with Glenn Beck. Oh, I could watch you two lob the ball back and forth all day.*] I laugh about Kathy giving it to me, and her looking at the camera for her show and pointing at me, saying, "Bill, this is your demographic! Your only demographic! Are you happy?"

Anyway, I got a big bang out of that.

Would I love it if Bill put Kathy's picture up as a "Patriot" at least once? Of course. Because Kathy is a patriot. The stuff she's done, going to Iraq and Afghanistan, performing for the soldiers, visiting the wounded at Walter Reed, I'm very proud of her. Kathy has nothing against this country. She loves it. So if you're reading this, Bill, I may have my own little chuckle when you correctly label her a "pinhead," but there's another side to her, too.

I do honestly hate it when journalists or writers can't see the other side of something. You have to do that to get the whole picture. I used to listen to Rush Limbaugh, but he's gotten so far off base, so unbalanced about things. It just seems like hatred. [*I was wrong, God. You do exist.*] Again, you'd think I followed every word Rush says, if you listen to my kids. Or that I never listen to anybody liberal. That's not the truth. I think.

I like that Rachel Maddow on MSNBC. I used to listen to Air America on the radio, even though I thought they were so far left, the names they called President Bush were disgusting. I really mean it. [*Especially when they called him "President." Ick.*] But I like Rachel's show. She's fair and balanced. [*I'm sure she'd love that you're using the Fox slogan to describe her, Mom.*] Rachel's a liberal, but I don't think she's nuts. [*Well, that's the important thing, Rachel. That you're not a raving, drooling lobotomy candidate, according to my mother's medical journal.*] She's really smart, and she never denigrates anybody who comes on her show, and I love that. Even if who she's talking with is against her. [*Yeah, it's called being civilized, as opposed to Glenn Beck wearing his plastic Hitler mustache yelling at a picture of the White House press secretary.*]

As for Keith Olbermann, I hate this little feud that he and my boy Bill are carrying on. Bill's always Keith's "Worst Guy Ever Around" or whatever the hell it is, and Keith is always a target of Bill's. It's childish. Honestly, guys, you're men. You're not little kids. Forget it already and move on to something important. [*Sounds like Judge Judy needs to open her docket for a Very Special Case.*]

Speaking of somebody who does important things, I do love that Anderson Cooper on CNN. First of all, I admire him so much for what he does, going to all those places like Iraq and Rwanda and Haiti and where the tsunami hit. Before anybody knew who he was, I'd see him in all these places and think, "Who is this guy?"

Plus, I thought he was so cute! [*God, Mom, you're so much more shallow than the other sophomores. I hate this sorority!*] He's also very smart and very serious, and you can tell he has a great sense of humor. And that's not just from being willing to stand there with Kathy on New Year's Eve when she's saying all those reckless things. [*Exhibit A: "Hey buddy, I'm workin' here, I don't go to your job and knock the dicks out of your mouth!"*]

The funny thing is, when I mentioned to Kathy after their first New Year's Eve appearance that I really liked him, she said, "Ma, don't you remember Anderson?"

"No," I said.

"From the show I did back on MTV?" she said, trying to jog my memory.

Oh, right! See, Kathy once had this show called *A Really Really Reality Show* [*actually, it was called* Kathy's So-Called Reality, *but whatever*] where she talked about reality TV. This was back when shows like *Survivor* were first starting to hit big, and Kathy wanted to have some fun with this new kind of television. Johnny and I used to be on the show with her—sometimes we read her mail on the air, or acted out scenes from reality programs, very funny stuff—but what I'd forgotten was that Anderson had been on, too! He used to host *The Mole,* after all. This was before he went to CNN.

One time, during a break, Johnny and I were sitting with Anderson and talking, just the three of us. We were asking him all kinds of questions, 'cause we didn't know him from Adam. "Are you in the biz?" "Do you want to be an actor?" Real innocuous stuff like that. [*I'm cringing so hard right now I'm not gonna crap for two months. Please tell me my mom did not turn to Anderson Cooper and say "Are you in the biz?" I was wrong, God. You don't exist. I'm back to being an atheist.*]

He said, "No, actually I want to be in the journalism business. I took some time off from that for a while because I wanted to get away from news and see what reality TV was all about. I've been having fun on this show here, for instance."

"Yeah," we said. "It is fun, isn't it?"

"But I think I'm done with this," he said. "I've had my taste of being out here, and I think it's time for me to go back and get into serious news and journalism."

We thought he was so nice and smart, and we wished him the best. Again, we didn't know who he was except a handsome fella with nice manners and what seemed to be a good head on his shoulders. So later Kathy came up to us and said, "You know who Anderson Cooper is, don't you?"

"I know he's on TV," I said. "He hosts that great show *The Mole*. But otherwise, no."

"Ma, he's Gloria Vanderbilt's *son*."

Oh Gosh, I darn near *died*! And here we were asking him about whether he wanted to be an actor! I was mortified. [*Thank you, Jesus! I'm back!*] But after I thought about it for a second, I told Kathy, "Thank Christ you didn't tell me that before we talked to him."

You know why? Because while Johnny would have been simply great talking to him with that knowledge, I would only have wanted to ask him about his mom. See, before she became known for fancy jeans, Gloria Vanderbilt was the daughter of a shipping magnate, and at a very young age—this would have been the early 1930s—she was involved in a custody battle between her mother and dead father's sister that was all over the papers. The country was immersed in it, and when I was a kid I followed it completely. She had always looked so adorable, wearing such cute little outfits and sporting those fancy bangs, kind of a Buster Brown look. I remember thinking what she had to go through was awful, and I felt real sorry for her. I've just always been fascinated by her. I even have her most recent book at hand, called *Obsession: An Erotic Tale*. It was a gift to Kathy from Anderson, autographed by Gloria herself! Never in my life did I think I would have a book on my coffee table autographed by THE Gloria Vanderbilt. What Kathleen doesn't know is that she left a note from Anderson inside the book that he wrote to her after New Year's Eve. I guess he had sent her some cookies and a pie from his favorite New York bakery. In the note, he calls it "crack pie." Gee, I hope he was kidding. [*Yeah, Mom. You caught me. There's a bakery in New York called Crack Pie, and they serve pies filled with crack cocaine and ship them undetected to hotels in New York City, and Anderson Cooper is their biggest customer. No, it wasn't a joke at all. Anderson Cooper actually sent me a pie filled with crack, and I think you should spend a lot of time worrying about it. You might want to report it to your beloved Bill.*]

Anyway, I can't wait to read the book!

Can you imagine, though, if I'd known the family connection when I met that wonderful Anderson Cooper? I'd have talked his ear off about his mom and what I thought of her, and it probably would have been the last thing he wanted to hear about. I don't know if I even would have been as friendly. I might have been too distracted. After all, she is one of the great beauties of our time. But we had a great talk with him as it was, and it says a lot that during our conversation, he was just like anybody else.

Or so we thought! Still, you never would have heard him say, "Oh, I'm from New York. You've heard of my mother, perhaps?" [*Actually, I think that's what Norman Bates would say.*]

Anyway, I love him. I love how he reports. I like the questions he asks. He doesn't ask the stupid Hollywood–type questions that never make any sense to the situation at hand. It's never, "How do you feel about the earthquake?" What's somebody supposed to say to that? "Oh, I think it's just great!" Anderson will ask the serious questions, the ones that get real answers, and he has compassion. I love how he's keepin' 'em honest. [*Does he also go around the world* 360°?] I'm just thrilled Kathy's met him and that they've become friends. I hope they stay friends. I know he's Gloria's, but I like to think of Anderson as my son, too. He's a great guy. [*You've got that right, Mom.*]

THE MANY USES OF
RUBBER BANDS

Rubber bands, the ultimate accessory. Perfect for when a clip or a pin isn't handy. And here's why:

GREAT FOR HOLDING TISSUES TOGETHER. Use two bands, one for fresh tissues and one for used.

STORE YOUR BEST SCRAPS OF PAPER by folding, stacking, and wrapping them in a rubber band. Add a pen to the stack for writing important notes, and don't forget to write "VIP" on everything.

GREAT FOR BINDING YOUR PANT LEG OR SKIRT to keep from tangling when riding a velocipede (one of those old high bicycles the folks rode back in the day), but it also works for modern bikes.

PERFECT FOR HOLDING OTHER RUBBER BANDS in a handy bundle.

GOOD FOR EMERGENCY TRIAGE, as a tourniquet or to hold a compress of tissues to a wound.

TIP
IT!

CHEWING GUM IN A PINCH. This was just a rumor back in my day, but during the great gum shortage of World War II, you'd hear of kids who would wind rubber bands around some mint sprigs and chew on that for up to a week. I'm not recommending it, though.

I HAVE OTHER KIDS BESIDES
KATHY, PART 3

The story I want to tell about young Gary, I don't think he's going to like.

But it's so cute!

See, Gary was a pretty introverted little kid. Where other members of our family might have been more outspoken or talkative or quick to make everyone laugh, Gary preferred to stay quiet and choose his moment to speak. Then it'd be really funny, maybe even more so because it took so long for him to say anything.

Well, one day early in his grammar school years, I not only walked him to school, but I offered to help out as a playground monitor. The Catholic school always needed any parental assistance it could get, and I was happy to oblige. So when lunch rolled around, I kept an eye on all the kids to make sure nobody did anything goofy like leave the grounds or get themselves hurt.

My son Gary in a school photo, looking adorable!

ST. BERNARDINE
1956

But Gary wouldn't leave my side. "Go play, Gary," I'd say. "I have a job here. I have to walk around and watch the kids."

Then the bell rang, and in typically great Catholic school fashion, every one of those kids got in line without making a sound. (I always loved that!) As they walked in, though, Gary kept looking around for me, and when he caught my eye he gave me this look like a little lost dog, and he started crying. Nothing tantrumy, just a sad little cry.

When he got home from school, I said, "Gary, why were you crying?"

He looked at me and said, "I was crying 'cause I was momsick!"

Not homesick, momsick! Isn't that just darling?

I know Gary's going to hate that story. Boys hate it when you tell sweet stories about them. They want to appear brave and tough. So I guess I'll add that we weren't surprised when Gary became a lawyer because as he got older, he loved playing devil's advocate with his family on any legal issue. (Johnny loved teaming up with him to do that.) When he starts throwing in "whereas" and "therefore" as he's giving us some spiel on how the law does this when we think it should do that, that's when I'll go "Forget the lawyer lingo, Gar[e]! Can't you just say the law's wrong?" I think he gets a kick out of driving us nuts like that.

AN OPEN LETTER TO THE BASTARD WHO STOLE OUR SWORD

[*Oh no. The sole purpose of this book in my mother's eyes. Get ready, people.*]

Dear Little Punk,

Maybe you remember that summer back in the late sixties.

The summer you did a horrible, horrible thing.

It was a lovely and lively night at the Griffin house in Oak Park, Illinois. We were having a party, like Griffins do, and this happened with a lot of our parties—the word about it had gotten out. Perhaps you heard about it from neighborhood people, or from my kids talking about it at school if you were of school age (which I think you were), or you were just driving by that night and noticed a lot of happy, well-fed people coming in and out of our house.

You wanted to join in the fun. And why not? I knew our parties occasionally attracted crashers. That's because we threw great parties. Sometimes Johnny and I were able to shoo the crashers away.

Not this time, I guess.

MAGGIE GRIFFIN

Side entrance of our Oak Park house, where a vicious thief escaped!

Surely, you helped yourself to some chips, cheese and crackers, perhaps, and maybe some potato salad. Then you washed it down with a soft drink, or one of the beers somebody smuggled in. Well, let me make it clear, none of that was for you. But I was probably in the kitchen when you invaded our home, or I was talking to my husband in the living room, or forcing myself to be interested in one of my daughter's re-hearsed monologues from some damn movie.

Maybe I even saw you. We might have even met. You probably introduced yourself as a friend of my son Gary, who was in high school at the time and would have had a lot of his high school buddies there. If you did, that was a sneaky move. You little snot.

I imagine you then made your way down to the rec room, because that's where the action always was. There, you probably overheard lively conversation about everything from movies and music to politics and religion. But none of that mattered to you, did it? Because that's when you saw it.

Our family sword.

In 1901, my husband's father went to fight in the Boer War in South Africa, on the side of the Afrikaners against the British—like many a good English-hating Irishman—and this sword was the fine, heavy, beautiful weapon he brought back from that conflict. Long, slightly curved, with a big handle and its own sheath, it was proudly displayed on our rec room wall. This was a piece of our history, something we *wanted* people to see—from the turn of the twentieth century!—and never in a million years did I think I was doing something reckless by having it in the open while we were throwing one of our parties. That's how dumb and innocent we were.

And how cagey were you? Once your heart stopped racing from coveting something that wasn't yours—let's not even go into how many commandments you broke that day—you probably then noticed how easy it'd be for you to make off with our prized possession. Unlike a lot of homes then, where basement access would have meant going through the kitchen, we had a side entrance/exit. When we got that house, the side entryway was a good thing. We thought. Yes, kids could run in on snowy, slushy days and head straight to the basement without trudging through the house, but what it also meant was, we could never see who exactly was going in and out of our basement area. You would have noticed that, because you're a goddamn sneak.

If you'd taken two seconds to think about what our reaction would be the next day, maybe that little ounce of goodness that I believe is in every person, maybe even including you, would have stopped you in your tracks. Because I was just sick when morning came and we realized the sword was gone. We went over every ounce of that house, looked in every crevice, hoping and praying that one of us had hidden it as a safety measure. Our next thought was "Whoever pulled this prank will come to their senses and return it." I'm not saying we didn't have a lot of goofballs among my children's group of friends. I was counting on the thief having a guilty conscience. It's probably why I didn't do what anybody in her right mind would have done: put up flyers, get the police involved, make them check out all the schools.

See, when I was a little girl hanging out at my dad's grocery store, I'd notice when kids would steal a piece of candy or a chocolate bar. These weren't bad kids, I knew. I didn't want to tell on them.

But I'd wait for them outside.

"I saw you take that candy bar!" I'd yell as they came out, watching their eyes get real, real wide. "Next time you do, I'm telling my dad!" Then, the kicker. "And *he's* gonna tell your *mother!*"

Believe me, that candy they just wolfed down didn't taste so sweet anymore.

But I wasn't on the ball the night you showed up at our house, and I could kick myself. This was such an offense against our family and home, it had me fuming for a long time. Then the shame set in, because I don't think we ever told Johnny's family it was stolen. Any Griffins who came over and asked, "Where's the sword?" would get a terrible lie from us as a response. "Oh, we have it upstairs hidden away because one of the hooks it was hanging from broke," we'd say. I was afraid to tell them. They would have been furious.

But not as furious as I've been, and still am, with you. You little rat.

"Maybe it was a nutball who just threw it in a Dumpster," my daughter Joyce said to me once. If that were so, it would just kill me. But you and I know that wasn't the case. You knew what it was that night in our rec room: something special, something valu-

Johnny's dad, Patrick Griffin, whose Boer War sword was stolen from us.

able. You're probably reading this right now in your fancy library, where our sword is handsomely mounted on a wall with other precious items you've stolen from other people's homes. Did you brag about it today to anyone? How you pulled the wool over the Griffins' eyes? I'll bet you did. I'll bet you did just that.

Give it back! It's not yours!

Sincerely pissed off,
Maggie Griffin

[*I told you. Dear reader, let's sit with this for a minute. Just when I think my mom is a crazy ninety-year-old who can hold a box of wine like no other, she knocks me on my ass with something like this. I admit, I kind of wanted to make fun of her for including this insanely obsessed letter. But instead, her piss and vinegar at this age is, dare I say it, admirable. My open letter to the punk who stole the sword is: You might as well use that sword to stab yourself in the heart right now. Because you've been frickin' served, Maggie style.*]

I SWEAR . . .

You know what I can't get over? Kathy never swore in our house growing up. [*That you knew of.*] I'm not saying I didn't slip occasionally myself. [*Oh, this is going to be rich.*] Especially if I was mad. My kids like to tease me about how I could change on a dime from using one voice with them, then another as soon as I heard the doorbell ring.

The way it supposedly goes is: "I've about had it with you goddamn kids for Chrissakes, Jesus, Mary, and Joseph!" *Ding dong.* Front door opens. "Oh hi, Mrs. Schildgen!" Chat, chat, chat. Then the door closes, and Ma's back at it again trying to discipline the little rascals, and maybe not so genteelly.

My husband's brother Maurice swore a lot in our house. Not the "f" word, but a lot of "bastard" and "shit" and those kinds of words. [*My favorite uncle, btw.*] Usually he directed it at Johnny and me at parties when we were arguing politics. That was always kind of funny, watching the kids' uncle Moe in full flight, calling us "nitwits" and worse. In fact, a neighbor once said, "Gee, Marge, I'm surprised your kids don't swear a lot because of the way Maurice talks." But my kids didn't swear. At least not around me! [*Yep. You got it. For sure.*]

When I grew up, swearing was a big no-no. [*So were ladies wearing pants.*] Also, there were many more words you couldn't say, certainly not the way you can say them now all over the place without anyone batting an eye. I remember once when I was in grammar school, I was sitting in the grocery store with my dad, just talking, when the bakery guy came in [*after the butcher and the candlestick maker*]. I happened to pick up one of the previous day's rolls—because the baker was there not just to deliver new ones but take back the old ones—and I said, "Oh my God, this is so stale!"

THWACK! Next thing I know, Dad's whacked me on the arm!

"Don't you use that kind of language in this house!" he said.

I almost didn't know what I'd said, I was so shocked. Then I realized, "Oh, the 'Oh my God.'" You can be sure I didn't say it again. In my dad's presence at least! [*Yep. You got it. For sure.*]

Kathy did get to know my dad before he died—this was when she was still in school—and they did love each other.

Dad thought she was really funny and cute. "Kitten," he called her. But boy, if my father had ever lived to see Kathy's act, he wouldn't put up with that for a minute. He wouldn't have talked to me, either, for my putting up with it! [*Um, I'm sure Grandpa was great, but for the record, I would have thrown that roll at his noggin.*]

But I think of the kinds of words that were really bad back then—"bitch," "bastard," and anything taking the Lord's name in vain, like a certain daughter of mine likes to use [*I learned from the master*]—and it does seem like you can say anything now. Sometimes a girl will be called a "bitch" and it's supposed to mean something good! The "f" word is very acceptable now, bandied about and whatnot.

Sometimes we'd disguise a word when we could. "Shite" for "shit," "witch" when we really meant "bitch," and "friggin'" and "freakin'" for you-know-what. It helped make you feel like you were swearing, but not really, you know?

But Kathy doesn't do any disguising, does she? I guess that's what showbiz does to you. [*And my occasional Satan worship.*] When she started at the Groundlings, I had to get used to that kind of language real fast. Johnny and I did a lot of gulping. But you get immune to it. Sometimes—then and now—I know she's saying something dirty, but I don't entirely understand it, and really, I don't want to, so that's just fine. [*According to my mother, denial IS a river in Egypt.*]

Apparently, though, whenever a Groundlings cast member's mom or dad or aunt or uncle was in the audience, they'd tell one another, "Okay, let's really make it nasty! Let's make 'em all sweat out there." One of the guys there told me that once, and I said, "Oooh, you're all a bunch of devils!" But when you're around young people, who aren't bothered by all that, you learn to live with it. [*Fuckin' A right, you do.*]

MAGGIE'S CURSE WORD
DO'S AND DON'TS

First of all, there's a difference between swearing and cursing. Swearing is for when you bang your shin on the stairs; cursing is for when you really need to tell someone what's what or give them a talking to, or hope they go to the bad place down below.

GODDAMN—Forbidden. Only to be used in extreme circumstances, or when it slips out by accident.

DAMNATION—A fancier way of saying "Damn," almost like it's a country's worth of "Damn."

AWW CHRIST—Also forbidden. I never say this. Except . . . sometimes.

SONOFABITCH—If you prick your finger while sewing.

SHITE—That thing some people don't know from shinola.

BASTARD—Not something you wanted to be called in my day, but now it's perfectly acceptable, as in "I'm in a bastard of a job."

TIP
IT!

SLOB—Terrible person. Messy, poorly groomed. Similar to a bum but I guess we're not supposed to say "bum" anymore.

PUSSY—You'd better be talking about a kitty cat.

DREGS—The lowest form of humanity.

LITTLE PUNK—A dirty thief. See the letter I wrote to whoever stole our sword (page 164).

FOR CHRISSAKES—I never say this, either. That I remember. If you feel you must say this one, say "For cryin' out loud" instead.

ASSHOLE—Only for holidays.

CRABAPPLE—A real sourpuss. Today they say "bummer" or "downer."

FRIGG IT—A nice way of saying one of Kathleen's favorites!

THINGS THAT ARE A PAIN
IN MY FANNY

MAKING A BED. Nothing is a bigger pain in the fanny than making a bed, especially the bigger ones, because you gotta walk around the thing, making sure everything is straight and neat. You could go round and round up to five times on one of those big beds.

ANYTHING I HAVE TO DO ON MY HANDS AND KNEES. Especially at this age, an activity like scrubbing the floor or even getting down there to look under the bed for a pair of pantyhose is out of the question and not only a big pain in the fanny, but a pain in the back, too. Of course, scrubbing the floor is easier these days. Swiffer took care of that.

NOT HAVING TISSUES WHEN YOU NEED ONE. I know I say it often but getting stuck without a tissue when you need one for an emergency is a big pain in the fanny.

THE COMPUTER. That little whirring ball that's supposed to let you know your e-mail is sending is a real pain in my fanny when it keeps going and going and never stops.

IRONING is a pain in the fanny, especially if you're in a rush. I like to take my time ironing, because if you rush things it comes out a mess. If you're ironing in a hurry you might just as well not bother.

BUYING A GIRDLE. Finding one that's comfortable is a big pain in the fanny.

WASHING BLINDS is a pain in the fanny because I always cut my fingers on the damn things.

STORE CLERKS WHO DON'T KNOW ANYTHING. I was trying to find candles, and I asked a young man where they were. "We don't have any," he said. I walk over two aisles, and there they are! What a pain in my fanny.

SPILLS. When the kids were younger it seemed that as soon as I had all the food on the table, one of them would spill the milk or juice all over it. Everything gets ruined, the bread gets soaked, and it's a pain in the fanny to clean up. One glass of spilled pop seems like a gallon when you're mopping.

MY DAUGHTER. I love her, but she can be a real pain in the fanny. I'll speak to you further.

HOW THE REMOTE CONTROL
AND PROGRESS IN GENERAL
RUINED MY LIFE

*L*ike most people my age, I think the world hasn't changed for the better. [*God, Mom, I hope this isn't a thinly veiled reference to slavery. I want to go on record as saying all Griffins are against slavery. Except sex dungeons with Levi Johnston.*]

It's probably not really true, but you have to admit, a certain way of life has gone. Whether it's a decline in behavior, or gadgets that make you lazy [*or crazy*], or ridiculously high prices, I sometimes wonder how anybody can stand it!

Take the Music, Please

Take music. That changed real fast. [*Oh boy.*] By the time I got to like the Beatles, for instance, they weren't considered wild anymore. You look back now and think, Why were they shocking? Of course, when rock and roll first started hitting big, I was already a mom trying to raise children, so at first I didn't like it. [*It has been well documented in several studies from junior colleges in Illinois that rock and roll can impede good parenting.*] You weren't going to catch me listening to it while I was vacuuming or cooking dinner. [*As if.*] Rock and rollers dressed goofy, they let their hair grow, and they looked like slobs half the time. I didn't care for it, especially those dance moves, and some of the lyrics. Kinda suggestive! [*Mom, how do you think babies are made?*]

But you learn to weed out the bad stuff, and now even I like a lot of it. Like those Beatles. We grew to love them. [*Well, during the "growing pains" phase of that love, I distinctly remember my mother had a "No White Album" rule when my aunt Irene came over, because of a little song called "Why Don't We Do It in the Road." It ain't all "Hey Jude," Ma.*] Although somebody had to explain to me years later that "Lucy in the Sky with Diamonds" was about drugs. I wouldn't have known that in a million years. [*Did you think it meant "Lucille Ball in the Sky with Diamonds"???*]

As for other big names, I never did like Elvis Presley. He was probably a decent guy underneath, but he just seemed like a hillbilly to me. [*Did she just write "hillbilly"? Now I'm going to have to do damage control with the Hillbilly-American community.*] Never bought his albums. Wasn't nuts about his movies. We would just laugh at stuff like "Hound Dog." *[Just pictured my mom and dad sitting together in the foyer holding a 45 of "Hound Dog" and doubled over with laughter.]* But his life turned out sad and pathetic. And that Mick Jagger of the Rolling Stones? Never a favorite. He was too wild, and looked dirty half the time. *[Ouch. I'm glad she's not on the board of the Rock and Roll Hall of Fame.]* And, oh God, not heavy metal. I don't get that at all. I can't even tell what they're doing with the instruments. *[She couldn't name three heavy metal acts if you put a gun to her head.]* And I never liked rap. There's no singing. I don't like the dirty ones, especially. Everyone's a "bitch" and a "ho"? Whatever they're saying, I know it isn't nice. *[Sorry, Luda.]*

Look, I'm not saying we didn't have our funny, silly songs in the big band era, which is when I was growing up. But nearly all our music was romantic. *[Nearly all is right, Mom. I don't think songs from that era like "Shave 'Em Dry," "It Ain't the Meat (It's the Motion)" or "Banana in Your Fruit Basket" qualified as "romantic."]* Songs were about the girl, finding her, not wanting to lose her, or if you lost her, getting her back! The music from my time was about longing for love, longing to keep someone. I loved it! *[Don't forget the longing for "fuckin'," as blues pioneer Lucille Bogan repeatedly sings in her 1935 recording "Shave 'Em Dry," which is dirtier than most gangsta rap. But I'm guessing Mom didn't make it to any juke joints back then.]* That's what Judy Garland, Bing Crosby, Lena Horne,

Rosie Clooney, and Frank Sinatra sang about: love and romance. Now, I'll admit I never did like Sinatra's personal life. But his talent, and the kinds of songs he performed? Wonderful!

Plus, back then we wanted to hear a nice voice, something pleasing to the ear. You know what I hate about music now? You can't hear the vocalist! The vocals get washed out by the darned drums [*I looked it up, and she's right on this one, drums were not invented until Elvis Presley was born*] or the wild guitars or all the computer noises. Hey, when I listen to music, I want to hear somebody sing! And the other thing is, I can never understand the words, either. Ever. But the kids all sure know them. From listening to it constantly on their iPods. Maybe I don't want to know the words to some of these songs.

By the way, I don't have an iPod. And I don't want one. [*NEWSFLASH: Apple stock plummets!*]

But getting back to what people in my day liked about music, what's changed is that the romance is gone. These days all the songs seem to be against the girl. It's crazy! I wish softer, prettier songs would come back. [*Maybe a song titled "I'm Not Against a Soft and Pretty Girl"? By Beyoncé?*] Then maybe young kids would realize it's kinda nice to be in love. [*Just ask young person Rihanna.*] In a *nice* way. Girls could feel that a guy is gonna protect you, and love you, and think you're the best person who ever lived. [*That's how stalkers think, Mom.*]

God, Yes, I Love Uniforms

Now, if you want to see me go into a tantrum, talk to me about children's clothes today. They're so sexy, for God's sake! These are kids we're talking about! [*Mom, cut it out. I'm thirty-two years old. Geez.*] Everything on them now is so tight, and usually real short, and tries to emphasize what little bosom half of 'em have (or don't have). [*I'm confused. So now you're pro implants for preteens?*] I wish you could see me rolling my eyes now. I swear, these kids don't get a chance to be teenagers anymore. They're boosted into the adult stage of life way before they're ready. [*Admit it, that's gotta hurt, Miley.*]

In my era, kids stayed kids until the first or second year of high school. Girls were still dumb and innocent and would giggle around the boys. [*Thanks, Gloria Steinem.*] Now the girls all act provocatively—thanks to these teen movies that drive me out of my mind [*the last teen movie Mom saw having been* Tammy and the Bachelor]—and the boys, well, I just want to slap them all in the face. [*Calling my attorneys now.*] They don't need the temptation. Boys are bad enough as they are, for Chrissakes. The ones who wear their pants halfway down their legs are so stupid-looking, too, I don't even know how they can think it's attractive. It's dumb. Dumb, I tell ya. [*I have to admit, I get warm and fuzzy feelings inside every time I think of my mom and dad sitting me down, screaming at me, "ALL MEN ARE PIGS!"*] And letting the kids wear caps in

TIP
IT!

schools, that's just so goofy. There's no teaching kids these days how you should dress properly. I don't think it's asking a lot to teach them that.

You might be able to tell from the above that I'm all in favor of uniforms. God, yes, I love uniforms. [*Mom, you have no idea how many men reading this book also love a man in uniform.*] They're what my kids wore when they went to Catholic grammar school and high school, and it made all the sense in the world. It relieves the kid of figuring out what to wear, and it cuts everybody down to the same size. We may have all cried about them when we had to wear them, but when there'd be those few weeks when you'd go to school without uniforms—and no, I don't mean without any clothes; you'd go in your own clothes while new uniforms were ordered— you were always glad when you had to go back to the uniform, because most of us didn't have anymore clothes to wear! There'd always be those few girls who had tons of clothes, but as I said, uniforms really equalize everyone. They take the focus off fashion, and put it back where it should be, on being clean and decent and hard-working. [*Here's the deal: As a mom of five kids, clearly she liked us wearing uniforms because it was easier for her. And Maggie being the youngest of sixteen children, clearly her mother loved uniforms because it was easier. Got it?*]

Besides, kids nowadays are so obsessed with brands! Everything has to be a brand name. It *kills* me to buy a brand name. The reason young people want them is because of all the advertising they see, everywhere they go. In my day you didn't have brand names. The papers would have advertisements that just showed you the dresses, or the jackets, and you didn't see designer names. You knew the name Levi's, I guess, for dungarees, and OshKosh B'Gosh, for overalls. But you wore those for manual labor. Guys never wore jeans for just hangin' around, like they do today. I blame television.

Home Entertainment Tonight

Speaking of television, when Johnny and I started raising our family in the 1940s, television was new, and a pretty exciting thing to get, I have to say. When I was a child, home entertainment was a wireless radio you listened to, or the wind-up Victrola for playing records. And getting the Victrola that plugged in was a big deal. But when television arrived, that was great. We all watched it together as a family. Those early sets were terrible, though. Half the time your picture was snow. [*If it was the news reporting a blizzard, you'd never know it.*] If you got a picture, you'd watch anything, you were so thrilled. I remember friends of ours who were fascinated by just the signal screen, that card that just indicated you were getting a signal. They'd watch only that if they could. [*Another glass of wine, anyone?*]

When the remote control came along, though, I have to say, I didn't want that. It seemed awful to me not to just get up and go over to the set and change the channel myself! [*My mother's early version of a personal trainer.*] I didn't get remote controls at first. I thought, "Now, that's just pampering." But I'm ashamed to admit, I love them now. Although these new remotes are more than a little confusing. There are so many buttons! What happened to just "On," "Off," "Volume," and little arrows for going up and down the channels? I can't figure these new ones out half the time. The other night I was trying to get to the Home and Garden network but somehow got stuck on Telemundo. [*Busted. I went over there and put it on Al Jazeera and left. I gotta have a little fun with the old gal.*] I gave up and just left it on there for the night. It begs the question, Why can't I just have the channels I want? It'd be like going to a restaurant where they just bring out everything on the menu, and you've got to find your dish. Half the channels they give you aren't even worth watching. Honestly. I watch Bravo, naturally, always wanting to see Kathy. And of course, Bill O'Reilly and *Judge Judy*. I like PBS. But so many network shows are nonsensical. The comedy is all toilet humor, suggestive and degrading. [*Not unlike* The O'Reilly Factor.]

And what's happened to the news? It's all Hollywood stuff now. [*That's why it's called* Entertainment Tonight. *Because the news is so fresh, it's from TONIGHT.*] It's all a tabloid. They pay attention to stuff that isn't even important! When I hear a newsman on a news show say, "The whole world is waiting to see if Brad and Angie are splitting!" Excuse me, but the whole world? With earthquakes happening? And wars going on? With the economy in the state it's in? My God, I don't think guys without jobs are waiting to see whether two movie stars are calling it quits. It's just awful and sad.

Not about Brad and Angie.

About the news.

Now that I think about it, my initial resistance to using the remote was also what happened with the clothes dryer. I never wanted one. I had a washing machine, and thank God, I was happy with only that, 'cause we had a good, warm basement, and a nice backyard. So hanging clothes was fine with me. [*I'm filing a lawsuit against my mother for fraud right this minute. I cannot recall one instance when my mother described the joy of doing laundry. I seem to recall "Johnny, help me fold this gah-dammn laundry! Holy SHITE, why did we have five gah-dammn kids? I'm EXHAUSTED." Or something to that effect.*] They'd dry overnight, summer or winter. [*You mean in Forest Park, Illinois, where the winters meant a wind chill effect of −17 degrees?*] But when I got a dryer finally, there went that pleasant time outdoors in the sun, putting clothes on the line. Sometimes I'd get the urge and put clothes out anyway. But it was a new era: I'd gotten spoiled. Let the dryer do the work. All I have to do is fold 'em. That's what we've come to. [*Come to think of it, she and my dad were always big on hanging rags. To this day, you can go to my mom's apartment, and no railing is safe.*]

Believe me, when I get these new contraptions like a remote or a dryer, I'm usually very happy eventually. But I'll
fight them at first. For as long as I can.

All the New Technology, LOL

You can probably guess how I felt about getting a computer.
[*Like bamboo shoots under your fingernails, maybe? Or worse???*]
One Christmas about ten years ago, Kathy surprised us. While
we were out, she had one installed in our home. We knew she
was expecting a call from us when we got home and saw this
fancy new gadget, so we phoned her with excitement in our
voices: "Oh my God, we got a computer!"

And we *were* excited.

But leery, too. Real leery. [*Like a first date with a serial
killer.*]

Because, see, it represented something we didn't need.
[*Like information.*] Why did I need a computer? "Oh, you'll
love e-mailing," my kids would say. Well, I like to write cards.
Cards somebody can in hold her hand, that say something nice
you wrote with *your* own hand. And I like to talk to people
personally on the phone. You want to hear people's voices
sometimes, you know?

Not that I wanted a cell phone, either, when you started
seeing everyone talking into one on the street. But even I had
to admit they're good to have for emergency purposes. I have

a nice little cell phone myself now, although I still don't know how to use the camera part. [*Or the phone part. She screams into that damn cell phone like she's mad at it. If you see her in a coffee shop, run.*] And honestly, I don't want to learn how to take a picture with it. Yet, what would I do if I saw Bill O'Reilly on the street? Oh geez.

Now, though, it's all about this texting, and tweetering. [*It's called twatting, Mom.*] My daughter Joyce, who's a wonderful teacher, said to me once, "It was hard enough to teach kids proper English and spelling when they *didn't* have texting. *Now* what is it going to be like?" [*Not to mention the semiautomatic weapons and the sexting and the cyberbullying.*] Kids aren't doing what I'm doing, which is consulting a dictionary every time I send an e-mail. [*She's describing spell-checking. She just doesn't know it. There's another computer setting she also does in real life. It's called "sleep." And she's up to about sixteen hours a day.*] There I am wondering, "Is that two 'r's?" while everyone else is writing "r u gng 2 lol" or whatever it is they abbreviate. It's got to hurt the spelling cause.

But Kathy and the rest of my kids have pulled me into the twenty-first century. When I first moved out to Los Angeles, whenever I'd see something in the *Los Angeles Times* that referred to Chicago, I would cut out the article and mail it to someone back in Chicago, who'd maybe copy it and give it to family members. [*What she really did was compulsively clip articles from any and every periodical about anything slightly Chicago-related, and the occasional Dear Abby column, and mail them to me.*

Oh, and by the way, Mom, stop with the articles about beloved family dogs dying a slow and horrible death. To this day, she'll send me a clipping from some old lady magazine titled something like "Saying Good-bye to Buster," with her handwriting in the margins, "Does this sound like your dog or what?" Eww!! No!!] But when we got a computer, Joyce had to say to me, "Ma, don't bother with the clippings. They can get the article on the Internet. Just e-mail them where it is, then they can call you and say, 'Oh, I read that article.'" That certainly saved a lot of postage. [*By the by, nothing pisses off old people more than stamps going up a penny.*] Of course, I don't really like reading newspapers on the computer. My eyes aren't that good.

I may have started out leery, but you can probably tell where this is going. Whaddaya know, like everything else, I got to using that computer, e-mail and everything, and now I'm pretty decent at it. [*If you consider calling the computer "a yellow pages that moves" getting pretty decent at it.*] But I have to say, what's this obsession with getting new computers when the one you have works just fine? [*She's got me there. I never really got over my Sharp Wizard.*] The kids wanted me to get a brand-new computer recently, because every time any of them was over here, they'd go nuts using the e-mail because it was so slow. "Well, it's fine for me," I'd say. "I'm not going anywhere anyway!" [*Why does that make it okay to wait AN HOUR for an e-mail to send?*]

Then Kathy got me a new one, and of course I love it. So much for "use it up, wear it out, make it do." Although when it heats up, I swear it's going to burst into flames. Do you think it will? I'm telling you, I'm afraid of these things. Are they really supposed to get that hot? It's like a radiator sometimes. [*Why don't you dry your laundry on it?*]

I guess the true indication of how much I've changed is that I'm even—gulp—sending *e-mail cards* now. I swear, sometimes I think I'm getting to be a bad person! What's happening to me? [*Okay, this is embarrassing. I don't know how to send an e-mail card. Touché, Mom.*]

Old-School Discipline

Sometimes, though, you have to look at what's always been accepted and maybe make some change yourself. Especially if it's about taking care of your kid.

My kids all went to Catholic grammar school. Three of them even went to Catholic high school (not Kathy, who insisted on public school) [*Thank you, Jesus*], and two went to Catholic colleges all the way through. And the one thing that Catholic schools did was instill manners and discipline in you. Those are two things all kids need, believe me. Parents need all the help we can get where discipline is concerned. I was happy with the Catholic schools. But what those schools typically meant was, you never blamed a nun or a priest for anything. And you certainly never went home and told your parents if you thought you were getting a bad shake, because they'd just say, "You're supposed to do what you're told, so behave yourselves." My dad wouldn't even listen to us if we griped about what went on at school. You might just get in more trouble if you did!

But what's most important, I came to realize, is sticking up for your kids when they're right, and once, I did have occasion to talk to a nun about Kathy. This was when she was in sixth grade, maybe seventh. A mother of one of her classmates called me one day and said, "Marge, I want to tell you something, and I think you should do something about it. It's about Kathy."

This surprised me. Kathy? My skinny, happy, curly-haired little cutie? See, I'd never had a single phone call about Kathy all through school so far. She was a wonderful kid. Really. As I always say, I've had more trouble with her as an adult than as a kid. [*It's called being a late bloomer.*]

Anyway, this mother said her daughter had come home from school and told her that if this one nun didn't stop picking on Kathy, she was going to stand up and really tell off that nun. "I'm gonna really tell her," this child was telling her mom. "I'm gonna say, 'Leave Kathy alone! All you do is pick on her!'"

I knew nothing about any of this. But apparently, it was bad enough that this nun would have Kathy crying and everything! Well, once I'd heard this from the mother and her daughter, I decided I had to call the nun that night. I gave it a lot of thought. It hurt me so much, I had to call. But boy, did it weigh on me. A whole lifetime of believing that you didn't talk back to teachers, nuns, priests, neighbors, or anyone in authority was rearing its head. But then there was the thought of Kathy, never even telling me what she'd been going through. That was what hurt so much.

I picked up the phone and called her. I tell ya, my whole body was shaking. And I was a grown woman in her fifties! I didn't scream. I didn't yell. But I wanted to know what this was all about.

"Does Kathy do anything to cause it? Not do her home-work, maybe? Because she's doing it here at home every night."

"No."

"Is she bad? Does she sass you?"

"No."

This sister had no excuse, and she barely tried to defend herself. She was just apparently one of those nuns who, if they can bully you, they will. There are people like that. That just makes me furious. Well, I told this nun in no uncertain terms, "You are a disgrace to the sisterhood. You should never have been a nun, and if this doesn't stop, I'm going much higher than this."

When I hung up the phone, I was still trembling. My hands were just quivering. I was ready to cry. Nowadays it seems like all parents do is blame teachers for whatever's going wrong

How could you let a nun bully this cute little girl?

with their kids, but what I did with that phone call then was going against my own personality, against everything I'd been taught. I just thought, you can't treat my Kathy like that, or any of my kids. That's the bottom line. It was so unfair, what this woman did.

Later, I asked Kathy about it. "How's Sister so-and-so treating you?"

"She's okay" was all I got.

She never complained about it, which I find very odd. I often wonder if what happened with that nun maybe traumatized her a little bit. But at least I found out from other kids that the nun never said one more word to Kathy. In the end, I must say I was so pleased with myself. I felt like a good mom! It also let me know that in certain situations, questioning authority doesn't have to be a bad thing. In that instance, I changed for the better.

[*P.S. I can now reveal the nun's name. Sister Mary Elizabeth Oprah Winfrey. Thanks, Mom!*]

TIP
IT!

PLACES THEY WON'T FIND YOUR BODY FOR DAYS

There are certain places on this planet that should be avoided at all costs, especially after ten o'clock. If you ever visit one of these Bermuda Triangles of everyday life and something happens to you, prepare to be lost until they broadcast the discovery of your lifeless body on the news, most likely with your underpants showing. These are places I've always warned my children about; now, I can warn you, too, readers.

Any wooded area

The car of a stranger or someone you just met

Beaches, lakes, swamps, basically any body of water, including the public pool

Parks, parking lots, and parketerias

That fancy new mall everyone is talking about

Any and all parties or rock-and-roll concerts

Fraternities and sororities, no thank you!

Your "friend's" house

I HAVE OTHER KIDS BESIDES KATHY, PART 4

*M*y youngest son, John Maurice, was the kind of likable, sweet kid who threw himself heart and soul into whatever he was into, and it was adorable. His ability to fixate on things came as a blessing one time when he was really young and got a jelly bean stuck way up his nose. He was all panicky, naturally, and I called the local police because they were really friendly and helpful about that kind of thing. They wanted to drive him to the station and see if one of the firemen—whose station was right next door to the policemen's—could get it out. Well, all the trauma went away as soon as JM noticed the machine gun in the cop car. You'd have thought nothing else happened that day after we got back home.

"Ma, did you see that machine gun? It was so big!"

I thought that was pretty cute.

Like his roller-skating, which he started up in grammar

My youngest son, John Maurice, looking happy at the beach in Saugatuck.

school at St. Bernardine's and got completely wrapped up in. All the kids loved it, really. JM would go to the rink all the time. Then he decided he was going to operate his own rink in our basement.

Our basement had a concrete floor, and it was pretty large, which meant kids could skate around in that space easily. Then we gave him a little record player so he could play music. Well, pretty soon, when his love of roller-skating was in full swing, he started making signs to put up, as if he were running his own roller-skating operation!

He made a sign that said ALL SKATE and he'd have it up, even if there was nobody else around but him! Then he'd skate around—he was really good at it—and maybe after that he'd announce, "Okay, now, couples only!" And then he'd have a COUPLES ONLY sign ready to go.

It was so funny and sweet to hear from above. He'd really get into it.

"I said couples only, Jimmy!" we'd hear him yell out. "You can't skate alone!"

And this might have been when nobody else was down there! Kids and their imaginations. Sometimes John Maurice had friends over, of course, but a lot of times it was just JM himself, master of his very own roller rink. He took that commitment to whatever he did—sports, hobbies, school, then business—and always wanted to be the best at whatever he was doing. Now he's married, to a wonderful woman named Jennifer, and has two great children, my grandkids Claire and John.

I hope he doesn't think that story was too embarrassing. But he was so adorable! This is the stuff you love to remember about your kids.

TIP
IT!

MAGGIE FIXES THE MOVIES

I love moving pictures. I've been going to "the show"—as I called it then—ever since I was a little kid when our little neighborhood theater ran cowboy movies [*now commonly known as gay porn*], comedies, and harmless family movies every Saturday and Sunday. Whether it was John Wayne riding his horse, Bing Crosby crooning a tune, Bette Davis not taking some sleazebucket's guff [*I hate when my mom swears, sorry, everybody*], or Judy Garland looking all adorable, movies and movie stars gave me a lot of pleasure. As I got older and movies changed, I went along with some of the changes. You start out shocked, and then you get a little used to it, and then something else comes along to shock you. [*Like Gwyneth Paltrow's career before that weird goop Web site.*] But movies have changed in other ways, too, besides the fact that nothing seems sacred anymore. Here's how I'd fix the movie industry, if anybody bothered to listen [*and why wouldn't they*] to one of its oldest, most steadfast supporters.

NO MORE BLOCKBUSTERS—I hate most of these blockbusters, movies about dinosaurs and space and the end of the world. What would I care for that? [*Yeah James Cameron, you pathetic failure.*]

QUIT IT WITH THE UNREAL CASTING—Now, I *love* indie

*Lana Turner, a favorite,
who made movies when
they were better.*

movies because they're real, and they're true. You might see a
couple of pretty girls, but at least they're not being cast as
grandmothers. In Hollywood, a movie about a family might
have the gorgeous little teen, an adorable-looking mother [*or in
Bristol Palin's case, an adorable-looking teen mother*], and a grandma
who looks thirty-five or forty and is still damn good-looking.
Probably played by that attractive Heather Locklear. It's so unreal how beautiful everyone is! That's why I like English
movies. Mothers look like mothers, and grandmas look like
grandmas. Sometimes the lead isn't even pretty! [*Ouch, sorry,
Brenda Blethyn. I guess that BAFTA award looks a little dull now.*]

TIP
IT!

ONLY ANNETTE BENING CAN DO NUDITY—Have you ever noticed nine out of ten nude scenes are always women? Of course. What else is new? Not that I even want to see the guy full-frontal. I am not interested. [*Especially in that sticky, stinky Ewan McGregor, who smells all European probly.*] But there was a great movie from about twenty years ago called *The Grifters,* which had one scene with Annette Bening where she comes out and wow! How she ever did that scene I'll never know. Now, I didn't know who she was then, but she looked gorgeous. I thought she would have come out with a towel on, but I guess that's what brings people in. It wouldn't draw me to a movie. But she was so good in that, I couldn't really take offense at it. [*Someone's getting a gift basket from Annette Bening!*]

HOLLYWOOD MEN NEED A SHOWER—I know everybody has to be a sex symbol now, especially the girls. But the guys all look like bums, like they've never washed their hair, or shaved, or cleaned and pressed any of their clothes. I can't get involved with any of them. [*Quit calling her, Matthew McConaughey. She will not take your phone calls.*]

. . . AND KEEP THE MEN AWAY IF THEY'RE TOO HANDSOME—I don't like a guy who loves attention from the girls, but isn't nice to the girl he's with. Good-looking guys to me are so in love with themselves; I've never been attracted to them. Robert Redford? Good-looking. Not interested. See, my idea of a guy is Robert Young. He looked so sweet and cute and nice. I loved that when he smiled, he got crinkles around his eyes. He was married to the same woman for a long time, too, which always influences me. When I was a young girl— when he was making movies, before his TV days on *Father Knows Best* and *Marcus Welby, M.D.*—Robert Young was the kind of guy I wanted to marry, and the kind of guy I wanted for my youngest daughter. I even said that once out loud to an audience of a panel show about dating that Kathy was participating in. I stood up and said to the host, "I really would love for Kathy to meet and marry a guy like Robert Young." [*I've heard this my whole life. Can a dead person take out a restraining order? My mother is stalking Robert Young's dead body.*] Well, that comment went over like a lead balloon, of course, because every girl in that room was probably into scrungy musicians. [*Note to Eddie Vedder: my mother has renamed the grunge movement the scrungy movement.*]

BELA LUGOSI: 1, *TWILIGHT* MOVIES: 0—I don't even know what's going on with those *Twilight* movies. I have no desire to see them. But they're not my kind of movies anyway. I have an aversion to scary movies, ever since I saw *Dracula* as a kid. Besides, you can't beat Bela Lugosi. How could you? [*So you're Team Bela, Mom?*]

BETTER WRITING—Writers don't get the credit they should in Hollywood. I don't care how good an actor you are—and that goes for fancy award winners [*Kathy Griffin, multi-Emmy winner*] and pretty young things all the guys drool over [*Kathy Griffin, Grammy nominee*]—you can't make a good scene out of bad writing. Directors are important, sure, but get a writer who can write, and you get a good movie. Although that Meryl Streep can do anything. [*Amen.*]

LESS TOILET HUMOR—[*Uh-oh.*] It's not funny. A little of it goes a long way. What happened to satiric comedy that took you a second to get the joke? [*Yawn.*] Something that makes you go, "Oh!" and with a smile. Instead of "Disgusting! Let's leave." [*The phrase I hear from an audience member if I've done my job.*] Really, comedy doesn't always have to be ya-ha-ha or go for the big guffaw. Look at Mae West. I had no interest in her as a kid—maybe because the Catholic Legion of Decency didn't want us to see her pictures—but now I love her movies, because her double entendres are priceless! They're funny and suggestive without aiming for the gutter.

I GUESS SEAN PENN IS OKAY—I hate to say this, but Sean Penn is one of my least favorite people, as well as one of Fox News's. But you know what, I can't deny the guy is a good actor. I care about him when he's playing someone. Other times, when he's playing somebody who's not so nice, I can't wait to see him get his comeuppance. [*Dead Man Getting Comeuppance.*] He can play almost anything. Really, I don't think I've ever seen him be bad, as much as it kills me to say that.

ENOUGH WITH THE LANGUAGE—I remember what a big deal it was when Clark Gable said, "Frankly, my dear, I don't give a damn" in *Gone With the Wind*. How things have changed. It's almost unusual now to see a movie without the "f" word all over the place, and without nude scenes. TV's getting bad now, too, thanks to HBO. It's coarsening America, and I don't think kids can handle all this stuff. [*Fuck those kids. They'll be fine.*]

KNOCK OFF THE UNNECESSARY SEX—Just knock it off. [*Calm down, Mary.*] In my day, you'd see the couple go in the bedroom, the door would close, and then you'd hear thunder and lightning, or see curtains blowing, and we all got the picture. [*There was bad weather outside?*] But now, we don't always have to see the couple in some nasty embrace, and then linger, and linger. Okay, we know they're kissing, we know they're going to make whoopee, but I don't want to see it. I feel dirty, like I'm looking through a keyhole at something I have no business looking at. You can show they're in love with glances or hand-holding, or a nice hug. Cut that other stuff down, and then you're fine. [*Oh God, I don't even know where to start.*]

MAKE MORE MOVIES LIKE *THE BUTCHER BOY*—[*WTF?*] Sometimes you see a movie where you're so drained because it's so good, and everybody in the theater feels the same way, that nobody moves when it's over. Everyone looks at one

TIP
IT!

another, and it's just silence. Or maybe you'll hear a quiet "Wasn't that great?" I just love that shared experience. Well, when Johnny and I saw *The Butcher Boy,* that one killed us. It's this Irish movie about a poor wretch of a kid who has this rotten life, as hard as he tries to be upbeat about it. But his father's a violent alcoholic and his mother commits suicide, and when the bitch of a neighbor spreads vicious rumors, he ends up murdering the neighbor and then gets sent to an asylum. Everyone was just wrecked afterward, drained. That movie was just wonderful! [*The Catholic version of a musical comedy.*]

JOHNNY

*F*or a marriage that lasted as long as Johnny's and mine did, and had as much mutual respect and love as it did, I will say this: we sure weren't that generous to each other right out of the gate!

The first I knew of the Griffin family was Johnny's older sister Mary, who I thought was the prettiest girl in Presentation parish. Johnny's other sister, Peg, was cute, too—and perky and funny; she went on to raise five wonderful sons. But Mary was maybe the prettiest girl I'd ever seen. She had big blue eyes and softly wavy hair and a beautiful smile. She was a terrific dresser, too, and could wear hats, scarves, and jewelry with real style. We all adored her fashion sense. I didn't know her well or anything, but I sure knew her looks. One day my sister Irene and I were outside our church when she alerted me to a young man coming out of the doors. "Oh

Mag, see that guy?" she said. "That's Johnny Griffin, that beautiful Mary Griffin's brother!"

Naturally I wanted to see what he looked like. But what I saw was somebody short, with dark hair, and cute, but not drop-dead handsome like Robert Taylor, as I was kind of expecting from somebody related to the gorgeous Mary.

"Gee, you'd never know it," I said. "The difference is amazing."

Isn't that terrible to say?

Well, when I finally met Johnny, it's not as if he said anything all that sweet, either. I was working at the Form Fit Bra Factory in the returns department, my second job after graduating from high school, and it was a great experience. I worked in the back of the building, where we were left alone. It was just a boss, me, and a girl named Helen who did the repairs on the bras. Johnny, it turned out, worked in a separate department boxing up items for shipping, and one day he was visiting with Helen.

"Oh Johnny," she said, "this is Margie Corbally, but you probably know that because she's in your parish."

I expected to get an "Oh sure, I've seen her around." Instead, he looked at me and said, "No, I've never seen her before."

Well, well, well! Suffice it to say, I was mighty offended by that, because while I was no Mary Griffin, I thought I was still pretty hot stuff. I'd certainly had enough of the guys from other departments come down to check me out when I first started working at Form Fit. But still, we were in the same parish! (Although he did live on the other side of Crawford Avenue, and in those days, a big street like that often kept neighborhoods from crossing over and getting to know other neighborhoods.)

Anyway, after that introduction, I thought, "God, he must really think he's something."

Young people are so nuts!

Later in our lives, I liked to tease my husband. "Johnny, you got off on the wrong foot with me!"

"I didn't see you!" he insisted.

"Oh I know you," I'd reply. "You wouldn't give me the satisfaction of saying you saw me." Then we'd laugh about it.

But I needed convincing after that first encounter. Johnny's friend Catherine Jameson was his big supporter to me. "Oh Margie, he's a doll!" she kept saying. "So funny and so nice."

Well, I certainly wasn't agreeing with that. But what do you know, he was on the El with me every day going to work, and before long we got to talking a lot. He'd ask if he could walk me home from the El, which was only a few blocks. And, of course, it didn't take me long to realize he was the funniest guy I'd been around in my life.

Johnny could see the humor in everything. Now, he didn't tell jokes, and it wasn't lampshade-on-your-head behavior. But he had a keen grasp of what was funny in every little thing around him. His observations were priceless. You know how Kathy's humor is really all about what she notices in people? That was her father. He could make me laugh like nobody else.

He got along great with Irene and Rae when he met them through me, and one night he told us he could get his mother's car and, if we liked, he could drive us all to the show on Saturday night and for a bite to eat afterward. We said "Fine," and that was the start of the four of us hanging out and having a great time. We did that for quite a while, and it was really fun. One New Year's Eve, Johnny got the car to take us to a big party at a tavern. We had a wonderful time, but the car wouldn't start when we tried to leave. That meant walking home, and out of vanity I had chosen to wear high heels over what the cold weather dictated, which were galoshes. Well, Johnny knew how to wring fun out of even a bitterly cold, windy trudge home. We'd run into apartment buildings occasionally for warmth, and while the girls and I were dancing around to get the chills out, Johnny would ring about six buzzers on the box in the foyer. You'd hear people grumbling, "Who the hell's down there! What are you doing?" We'd be ready to kill Johnny as we chased him outside, but we were laughing really hard, too.

Of course, I was starting to really like him. But I didn't know exactly how he felt about me, because he seemed to enjoy being with all of us. Well, one night we were waiting for Irene and Rae because we were all supposed to go see a movie, and the word came that they'd been hung up someplace. I suggested sitting and waiting for them, but it would have meant missing the film.

"No, Mag," Johnny said. "Why don't just you and I go?"

I was so surprised. "Gee," I stammered out. "I . . . I don't know."

But I said yes. And it wasn't so hard to say, either. Johnny would later tell me, "Mag, I had been waiting for MONTHS for that to happen! I knew how you were with the girls, and I was afraid to call my hand too soon." How sweet!

That was when we started going out on dates by ourselves, and Johnny and I became a real couple. But I didn't have to feel bad for Irene and Rae. As luck would have it, Johnny had a buddy named Jim who fell for Rae, and around the same time, my sister Anne introduced Irene to an aspiring fireman named Joe who fell for her! Pairing off with Johnny might have even sparked these connections, too, because these guys suddenly felt they could ask the other girls out. We all fell in love with our eventual husbands at the same time, I tell you. It was strange, amazing, and perfect.

When war talk started building in 1940 because of what was going on in Europe and the Pacific, Johnny, who was twenty-four, did what a lot of young men did then: he enlisted. The feeling was, join up before you had to join, and you might be out in a year. Plus, you'd get your job back, with seniority. (By that time, Johnny was working for a shipping company.)

We'd talked about getting married, and we decided to wait until he got out of the army.

It was the beginning of December 1941 when Johnny got a furlough from the military, and I couldn't have been more excited. Spokane, Washington, where Johnny was stationed at Felts Field, had seemed so far away, and now I was going to have him home for three weeks!

It turned out to be only three days. It was a Sunday, and we were all getting ready for a big dinner that night at my sister Anne's, when they announced on the radio that Pearl Harbor had been attacked. None of us even knew where Pearl Harbor was. But we knew what it meant. Johnny had to go back. I was devastated. We saw each other at my sister's that night, anyway, but the mood was more anxious than celebratory.

It wouldn't be for another day or so that he could get back, anyway, because he had to get everything in order per the army's wishes. Plus, transportation options were few. But boy, it was thrilling to see how quickly this country acted. Everything became for the soldiers, especially the trains. If you were going somewhere, too bad. You had to wait until a seat opened up that wasn't needed for a man in uniform. Also, they started rationing food right away. You couldn't just buy sugar or butter or meat whenever you wanted. The way this country came together was wonderful.

But my Johnny was going to be gone now for a lot longer than we'd hoped. On top of his training to be an aerial photographer, he'd now get combat training, too. How did I know he wouldn't be shipped overseas immediately?

Johnny wrote me a letter when he returned to Spokane, saying he thought it was time for us to get married. As you might imagine, I was all for it. My dad wasn't so hot about the idea, though. He was always helping his grown kids if they had money problems, or if a grandchild didn't have one of his parents around because of divorce or death, so he imagined a future scenario in which he was once again helping out one of his children, in this case a widowed daughter with a young child—a sad scenario, sure, but a realistic one—and he just didn't see the necessity in us rushing into marriage. I could see his point. Most girls waited out the war to get married, but Johnny and I didn't want to wait.

But there was also something very attractive about making a clean break from our families. If we were in Spokane, we could start our lives without anybody telling us what we were doing wrong. As much as I grew to love Johnny's mother, for instance, she was a forceful presence who was used to raising her kids and telling them what to do, and she could sometimes be pretty hard to take. By ourselves, I'd be able to make a crummy meal for Johnny and nobody had to know but him.

So I went straight to Spokane, where Johnny had an apartment ready to go, and on the morning of March 20, 1942, we got married, with only an army buddy of Johnny's and his girlfriend to stand up for us. Nobody could make it out from

Chicago, because it was wartime, and traveling like that just wasn't easy. But I got two telegrams from my family, which was so thrilling, plus cards and money from both our families. Even Dad, who was so against it, sent us money, with a note: "Use it wisely." So we threw ourselves a nice breakfast afterward at the Desert Hotel to celebrate.

I was happy as a lark. I wore a simple but nice suit that was a real soft yellow with a corsage of purple violets and a hat and veil that were black. Johnny was in his army uniform. Johnny could be romantic when he wanted to be, but my favorite photo from that day is of him right before he has to sign the church's marriage registry. He's got this "Boy, what did I do?" look on his face, like he didn't know whether he wanted to sign or not, and I'm laughing like hell. It's so cute. The guys there were so funny about it, too. They kept saying, "John, we're waiting in line if you don't want her!"

Immediately we knew that getting married was the right thing to do. Our one-bedroom apartment in Spokane was cozy enough, and I made good friends right away in that building, one of them a pregnant girl whose husband was overseas. With so many people around me in the same boat, I never got afraid or anything, even the times Johnny might be at the base all night on duty. And while I always missed my family, I knew we were getting the best start for our marriage away from any potential criticism. And I didn't know how to do anything, really. The first time I washed a floor, I used so

Our wedding day: Johnny being funny, me laughing. I love it.

many soap suds that it seemed like I was rinsing and re-rinsing that surface for days!

Then our first child, Kenny, was born, nine months and five days after our wedding, which certainly pleased my father, I'll have you know. But it wasn't long after that that I took Kenny back to Chicago, because Johnny was being sent to Laredo, Texas, for more training, and he didn't think I'd want to follow him. "It's scroungy and beastly hot," Johnny said. "I wouldn't ask you to come here, Mag." I didn't notice any of the other wives going there, either. So I moved into an apartment close to my dad's store, with my sister Irene as a roommate.

Then Johnny was sent to Denver, and his commanding officer said it wouldn't be a bad idea for the men's wives to join them. I had to agree. Kenny was thirteen months old at the time, and I ended up loving Denver. Between Spokane and Denver—two gorgeous cities—I felt like I was luckier than a lot of other army wives. Rae's husband, Jim, for instance, was sent to Tullahoma, Tennessee. Let's just say Rae wasn't too keen on the place.

When Johnny's stint in the army was up, and we were finally able to settle down in Chicago, I realized that Johnny had never lived in a house—he'd grown up in apartments— and I, meanwhile, had lived only in houses until our early married days. I said, "Johnny, I want a house." He said, "Fine." We moved into a house one of my brothers had lived in, which was only a block away from my parents. We never suffered for babysitters, because Kenny was their first grandchild in a while, since their other grandkids had grown by that time.

When it came to child rearing, Johnny took to it like a pro. He never complained about changing diapers, or giving a bath, or doing laundry. He was really good about that. There was no henpecking going on, either! I just want to make that clear, in case anybody's thinking he was unhappy with sharing these chores. I simply got a great guy for a husband.

You want to know how great Johnny was? Because we were living paycheck to paycheck after the war ended—Johnny having gotten his solid but not-so-high-paying job back at Railway Express—we could only afford a house that needed a lot of work. (Really, every house we ever bought was like that!) At the time we moved into our first home, Johnny didn't know a whole lot about plumbing, carpentry, and so on. The most he ever did growing up, living in an apartment, was paint walls. But the guys he worked with knew all that stuff, and they were only too happy to show him. And Johnny took to it all beautifully. He loved learning how to build a fence, tile a floor, make dormers. The thing about Johnny was, whatever he concentrated on, he did right. That endeared him to Dad. "Such a fine young man!" he'd say about Johnny.

One thing we would always joke about was how useless I felt watching his workmates' wives help their husbands with all the fixing-up jobs. They seemed to know all about it, too! One couple was Polish, and another was German. And here I was, the Irish girl who—at the most—could be a gofer if he needed a certain tool or brush or a pail of water. But my abilities stopped at housework.

One day I said to Johnny, "Gee, John, you know who you should've married? A good strong German or Polish girl. They'd be working with you on those tiles, putting them down. They'd take on half the work! This Irish girl here is only handing you stuff."

TIP
IT!

That was always good for a laugh between us.

"She'd have the walls painted by the time you got home from work!" I'd say.

"I'd get a really hearty meal, too," he'd add. "Sausages and roasts and stews."

"A good cook *and* someone who knows how to make dormers!"

Then we'd take it even further, really exaggerate.

"Here I am," I'd say, "wanting you to stop and take a break, have a cup of tea and a piece of cake with me. She'd want to work straight through. Eight hours. Maybe a lunch break. But that's it."

It would end with a silly plea on my part. "If anything happens to me, John, don't make the same mistake twice and marry an Irish girl. Find yourself a nice strong German or Polish girl. You'll be a lot healthier!"

People want to know what the secret to our marriage was, why it lasted so long. I don't know if I have an answer outside of the fact that neither one of us liked to fight. We'd rather laugh and talk pleasantly. We also balanced each other really well. Where I would worry, Johnny would be calm. That's not to say we didn't have disagreements. But we knew how to talk about them. And laugh about them. There's nothing greater in a relationship than being able to laugh about yourself.

I think what we had was a way to see past a disagreement. When we first moved to the suburb of Forest Park, we bought a house that—you guessed it—needed work. One

Outside the Polo Lounge. Don't we look young, healthy, and rich?

day I decided to buy some new drapes, and Johnny offered to paint the dining room while I was gone. We'd already mixed the paint to get the color we wanted. I thought it was great that he was going to jump right into this big project.

I don't remember how long I was gone, but when I got back, he had a whole wall painted. "How do you like it, Mag?" he said excitedly.

Now, those of you who've done a paint job know that paint can be funny. You mix and mix, you get it to the color you want, but when you actually put it on the wall, it might not look like what you wanted. The light might hit it a certain way, whatever. Well, right then and there, I was looking at a wall color I didn't like.

"Aw, John, that's not what I wanted at all!" I said.

"But that's the color you—"

"I know, I know," I said. "But it should be more blue-ish. It's too gray!"

Then I said the words no husband ever really wants to hear. "John, do you think you could paint it over again?"

I expected him to come back with, "No, I'll paint the other walls to make it contrasting. We'll live with it." Because, honestly, that's what I would have said in that situation.

Instead, he gently replied, "Are you sure?"

I said, "Yeah, John, I really would love it to be that blue color."

"Okay. I'll do it again."

Really, how could you not love a guy who'll do that for you, and not complain? Of course, he did a great job, and it looked beautiful, and I couldn't wait to point that out to everybody who saw it. He was so good to me our whole life. When we were much older, I brought up the wall to him and said, "John, why were you so good to me?"

He laughed at the memory of it, and then he said, "You know why I did that, Mag? Because whenever I would do anything, you would be so happy about it, you'd say 'I love it!' and then throw your arms around me and kiss me. I loved doing stuff for you, because I got that reaction."

On top of Mount Spokane, and on top of the world.

That was the truth. I meant every kind word I ever said about Johnny. And I loved saying kind things about him. I don't know what else to say, really. I always felt really lucky to have him. Because a lot of marriages aren't happy. You see couples who love to fight, who love to fight in front of you, and I wonder, doesn't that take something out of you? Don't you tend to say things you regret? I loved Johnny too much, and I think he loved me too much, to do that. I don't know if people go into a marriage thinking it's going to be perfect, but what I always felt was, Johnny was perfect *for me*. And I hope I was perfect for him.

TIP
IT!

I've included in this book one of our favorite photos, from our wedding day. After the ceremony and our breakfast, Johnny had gotten a friend to loan him a car for the day, so we drove straight to Mount Spokane. It was a beautiful spring day in that part of the country—nicer weather than we were used to in Chicago—and we made our honeymoon out of taking in the view from the top.

I'm so glad we got a picture of that moment, holding hands, happy, ready to start our lives together. It's a photo Johnny and I often took out and looked at, and whenever we did, I'd always say, "We were on top of the world that day, Johnny."

He always replied, "Mag, we still are."

MAGGIE GRIFFIN

MAGGIE'S DATING RULES FOR A YOUNG GENTLEMAN OR LADY

RULE #1: Never get in an automobile. This means trouble.

RULE #2: Keep it under wraps. No need to dress provocatively and spoil the surprise. If it were up to me, young ladies would still be wearing high-collared blouses and buttoned shoes. And a bustle. A six-rib bustle, not one of those slutty three-rib kinds.

RULE #3: Don't overdo the makeup. We all know what boys want. No need to encourage them by appearing tarty.

RULE #4: No rock and roll. Too suggestive. You know what's nice to listen to on a date? Nat King Cole or that sweet Mel Tormé. At the most, Rosie Clooney.

RULE #5: Do not have sex. You're not married, for cryin' out loud.

TIP
IT!

LIFE IS A BOX OF WINE

*A**ttention anyone who is currently in AA, or any alcohol-
related treatment program: Do not read this chapter. It will
surely cause you to have what is called "a slip" in the Big
Book of AA. You have never read a love letter to booze like this in
your life. This is Maggie really letting loose. I've never had a drop of
alcohol in my life, but by the end of this chapter, I wanted to drink
something called a Tom Collins, and then I wanted to have sex with
someone named Tom Collins. Now, if you are someone who is able
to imbibe on a casual level, or feels like giving up on decades of sobri-
ety right now, this is your chapter. You have to be carded to even read
it. Bottoms up, kids!]*

Before I tipped it, readers, I sipped it.

I grew up at a time when cocktails and mixed drinks
were the rage. That's what my older sisters drank when they
went out, or were staying in their own homes with company.
(Never under my parents' roof, because Dad didn't keep

liquor there and didn't like women drinking, anyway.) These drinks my sisters liked had names like whiskey sour, Manhattan, Brandy Alexander, Old-Fashioned, Tom Collins, and, of course, the famous martini.

My sisters always looked so sophisticated with these drinks. Especially when they smoked, too. Boy, did I want to smoke. I thought it was the epitome of glamour and sophistication, and I loved imagining myself in a fancy restaurant holding a lit cigarette, like I was Myrna Loy or Claudette Colbert. But whenever I tried, I'd just hack and cough, so I said, "Forget it." That kind of glamour wasn't in the cards. (Dad hated women smoking, too. It was unladylike and meant you were "tough.")

I didn't have an urge to drink, though, even when I came of age. So when I started to date Johnny, and we'd go to taverns and hang out there for hours with friends while somebody played a piano and sang, I felt like I had to learn to drink to be sociable. I was tired of hearing, "You mean you're not drinking?"

Johnny was a beer man, but I never had a taste for beer—although a cold one always looked like the right thing to drink on a hot summer day—so what I picked out for myself was a highball. But you'd hardly call it an alcoholic drink. I'd order a tall glass that had a teeny little shot of whiskey, and a whole lot of ginger ale and ice. I didn't really like whiskey. By itself, it was dry and horrible and stuck in my throat. But I loved ginger ale. So I'd nurse my weak highball for four hours. One glass. Sip, sip, sip. The bartender always wondered how I even tasted anything. I know he meant the alcohol. But I tasted ginger ale at least!

My then-boyfriend, husband-to-be had the best response. Johnny always said, "Mag, you're a cheap date."

That always gave me a kick.

My first experience with wine came when my dad, who was a solid beer drinker, decided to take his doctor's advice and drink a little red wine. So when I'd go to visit him, I'd bring him a bottle of Mogen David, which is a cheap, really sweet wine. If you've never had it, I dare say there's hardly anything sweeter that comes in a bottle. My dad would sip his one little glass, and he'd pour me one, too. (I had to be married for Dad to offer me an alcoholic beverage.)

Well, I kind of liked it! Suddenly, a glass of Mogen David became my one drink for the night. If we went out for a sandwich, or even spaghetti, that's what I'd order. Of course, I knew nothing about what wine goes with what food, so if you're wincing, I don't blame you. Then I found out about sherry—a sweetish wine, but closer to being dry—and started to like having a glass of that.

Of course, what your friends drink often has an influence on you. So when Johnny and I started socializing with a group of people who liked cocktails, I came around to those drinks my sisters were enjoying. Occasionally I'd have a Manhattan, which appealed to my sweet tooth because you mixed whiskey with sweet vermouth, and it comes with a maraschino cherry. Then there was the Tom Collins, a favorite at our summer parties, which combined gin—or vodka, which I preferred, 'cause I found gin too strong—with lime or lemon, sugar, ice, and fizzy water. But what I liked most were Old-Fashioneds, which I've heard is the earliest known cocktail! An Old-Fashioned is quite the mixture: whiskey, seltzer, sugar, bitters, and orange juice. At least that's what mine had. Everybody has different recipes for an Old-Fashioned.

My brother Pat, who had a tavern in Chicago, made a great one. It was so great, in fact, I used his recipe to make an Old-Fashioned punch for our Christmas parties, which was a big hit when you were coming in from the frosty, snowy Chicago winter air. As soon as people entered our house, you'd hear "Where's that punch?" It was strong stuff. Two sips of that, and you were warm, I tell you! But you couldn't drink too much, and people would usually switch to beer or wine after a sampling of that concoction. I felt that way about Manhattans, too. I could never drink two in one night. Sugar with alcohol is a killer! I don't mind feeling a little silly because of a drink, but who wants to be dizzy? That's like being sick, and that's no fun. (Of course, in Kathy's estimation—since she never drinks—anybody who's had two drinks is shot. Which is when I tell her she doesn't know shite from shinola. What do you call someone who eats more than two pieces of cake at one time, Kathy?)

But it was when Johnny and I first visited Europe in 1974—Ireland, England, and France—that everything changed. Well, first of all, when we landed in Ireland, I cried because I never thought I'd ever get to see where my family was from. We visited my parents' church in the coastal town of Drogheda, met relatives for tea, and visited spectacular castles. Johnny drank the Irish beers he loved so much, and we had a wonderful time. (Although they weren't too keen on giving me more ice for my cocktails.)

In Paris, though, our fondness for "fancy drinks" ran into a wall. We might have figured that would happen. Here we were in this beautiful wine-producing, wine-drinking country, and when we'd go to the bar and order a Manhattan or an Old-Fashioned, nobody would have a clue what we were talking about. Johnny actually stepped behind the bar once to show the bartender how to make a Manhattan! Anyway, that was our tourist mistake, ordering mixed drinks in a famous wine country. Also, what we noticed was that the French were drinking wine all day long in these cute little cafés and bars, and they just looked so comfortable and relaxed and continental. So we said, "We'd better start ordering just wine."

Our trip instantly got better. (We saw Pierre Salinger on the Rue de Rivoli trying to hail a cab!) The wine was delicious, we had a wonderful time, and that's when we made the big switch.

Thank goodness my tastes evolved from my Mogen David days. I think I'm like a lot of people, in that I may not know a lot about wine, but I know what I like. People will ask me as they're handing me a glass, "How do you like this wine?" I hate to say it, but most of them taste kind of the same to me, especially reds. I'm better at distinguishing whites. Some are darker. Some are sweeter. Some are lighter. Some are drier. I very seldom have a wine I really don't like, unless it's really sweet. So I'm not a big fan of Riesling or Gewürztraminer. Or the ones you have with desserts. But I guess they're okay if you're having one with a cookie.

Chardonnay is my favorite, more than Chablis, which is what I used to drink. I've really gotten to like wine that's a little on the dry side. Something that's nice all by itself if you're just having a glass in the afternoon, maybe with some cheese and crackers, or that works with a meal. Another white I like is Pinot Grigio.

The markup on wines, though, can be a bit much when you go out. That's why Johnny and I liked happy hours. But even then, you have to be careful. One time we decided to try a new place near the Santa Monica airport that was very chichi, so we dropped in for happy hour and each ordered a glass of their house white wine from the bar. This was maybe ten years ago, when the top price for wine by the glass was maybe $9. So John puts a twenty-dollar bill down, figuring that ought to cover the cost and a tip, and as we're heading with our glasses to find a table, we hear "Oh, sir?"

Turns out the wines were $12 a glass!

We had a good laugh about it, but we looked at each other and thought, "We're not coming here often!"

That's why we were excited about a little discovery we made later when we went to a friend's yard party. Everybody was supposed to bring something, so I made a big salad. Well, this other guy said he'd bring the wine. At the party he started opening these reds and whites and began passing it around. None of us looked at the labels or anything. Then he asked, "How do you guys like the wine?"

We all thought, "Hey, this is good. It's nice wine!"

"Well, as long as you all like it, let me tell you about it. And wait till you hear how much it costs."

He said it was two dollars a bottle! We couldn't believe it. This was a guy who would think nothing of spending $40, $50, or $60 on a bottle of wine. He appreciates good wine. But he also likes anything that's drinkable, which I love. That's when we decided to start buying this wine, which was made by Charles Shaw. Then we started going to other people's houses, and you'd hear, "Hey, did you try this new Two Buck Chuck?" Now it had its own cute little name!

Look, this isn't the wine you save for special occasions. Friends of Kathy's will give me really nice bottles of wine, and those are like gold. You have to dole those out. You'd better be special if you're going to get me to open one of those. But Two Buck Chuck is good wine! I don't know of anybody who's gotten sick on it or anything. I'm sure it's not the favorite of wine snobs, but if they don't want to drink it, fine. If one came to my house, I'd even go out of my way not to serve it to them. Why give them the satisfaction of trashing it? (I might even be sneaky enough to pretend I don't drink it either!)

But you can't fault that price. Especially since you can go to Europe and sit in a cute little outdoor café near a vineyard and order their house wine, and it's the equivalent of two dollars, too! And it's good! And Europeans know their wine.

Which brings us to the box.

That was another revelation. When we learned about box wine—again, from friends whose house we were at for a party—everything seemed to fall into place. All the pesky little problems that come with wine from a bottle were solved by that box.

First of all, when you open a bottle of red, how long is it going to last? Not long, I'll tell you that much. You'll have vinegar on your hands if you don't drink it all in a day or two, and for someone like me who has a glass or two at a time, that's a lot of pressure. Well, that box keeps it from going bad for a long time! Of course, the box itself isn't keeping the wine. That would be strange, to say the least. It's a plastic bag inside the box. But it's a special vacuum-sealed bag that keeps air out, which is what starts the process of turning wine bad.

Then there's the spigot. How convenient is that? Especially on a picnic, say, when you might be kicking yourself if you brought a bottle of wine but forgot a corkscrew. But even if you're at home, you just prop that box up on the counter, or on a shelf in your refridge, and you can get a glass quickly and easily. Less chance of spilling, too!

Best of all, the value of getting the equivalent of three to four bottles in one box means it's the ideal way to bring wine

*Me and little Kathleen,
before she learned to
swear.*

*Joyce and me at a
banquet dinner,
tippin' it!*

*Me and Irene on the
left, casual, and Rae's
all dolled up.*

MAGGIE GRIFFIN

In Chicago with John Maurice's family: wife Jennifer, grandkids Claire and John

Having fun with Team Griffin: Tiffany, me, Kathy, and Tom.

Below:
Christmas 2004. BACK ROW: *John Maurice and Gary;* MIDDLE: *Kathy, Claire, Johnny, me, and Joyce;* FRONT: *Jennifer and John.*

to a party. Try lugging four bottles to a party. They're sliding around in your car, clanking against one another. They might break. They're heavy with all that glass. It's two trips from the car, surely, especially if you brought a big salad, too. A box of wine with a handle takes care of that inconvenience!

Don't let anybody tell you that box of Franzia or Almaden is empty, either, just because that spigot runs dry. There's always a little more.

That's when you call out, "Tip it!"

In other words, use it up, wear it out, make it do!

Then again, isn't it nice that "Tip it" also acts as a toast? Even a way to view life? Over the years I've had the pleasure of tipping it with Johnny, my kids, family, friends, and even by myself, especially when I want to relax after a hard day of worrying about what latest controversy my daughter has gotten into. Hey, Kathy may not drink, but she tips it, wouldn't you say, when it comes to her comedy? She probably wouldn't be as successful as she is if she didn't.

As a motto for living life to the fullest, and getting the most out of it, I think "Tip it!" works pretty well. And at ninety, I think I deserve a motto, don't you?

What's yours?

TIPS FOR TIPPIN' IT

As you know, I love my box wine. Here are some reasons why:

A box is more convenient. You don't need a corkscrew, you can reseal the thing, and it stays fresh longer. Plus, a box won't shatter and cut your hand. Nobody ever got a cardboard paper cut.

A box is easy to store, you can stack the darn thing, it's a box, for cryin' out loud!

Irene and me tippin' it. You could say I'm in a semi-duster.

TIP
IT!

A box holds four bottles' worth of wine. I wouldn't bother with those measly cartons that hold only a bottle or two's worth.

A box has a spigot. Not only is it resealable as I mentioned earlier, but a spigot doesn't spill.

A box instead of a bottle is greener! It reduces your carbon footprint! Whatever that means.

A box is perfect for home and family and large parties. Fancy bottled wine is for intimate occasions and company. But only company you like. Certainly not for anyone uninvited, or crashers.

And remember, Tip it! You may think there's no more, but try again. You'll be sure to get the last drop.

Johnny and me tippin' it. I couldn't tell you where this is.

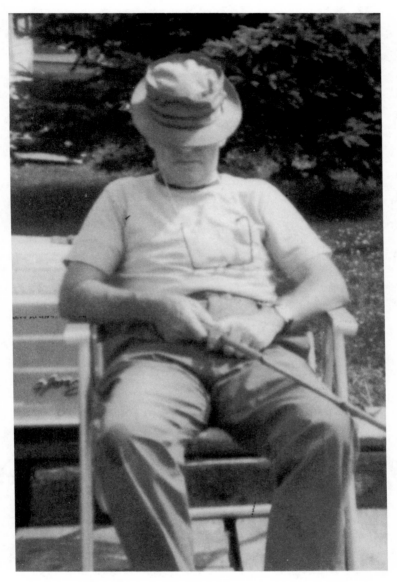

Johnny in his favorite golfing/shopping/waiting pose. Yes, he'd actually nap!